"Words cannot b
truly enjoyed reading
spine, and goosebum
experienced when rea
. . . My hope for you is that after reading this book, you'll be
inspired to embrace your 'weird' too."

-Amy Grafe, Usui Reiki, Karuna Reiki® Practitioner

"Eloquently and authentically written! Kady provides
some of the most real and magical moments of her life, sharing her unfiltered struggles along her path to discovering herself and the beautiful gifts she has to offer. This heartfelt quest
to tap into a greater unknown will have you hooked!"

-Brittany Rothwell, Wellness Coach

"Such a great read! I could not put it down! I fell right
into the story with moments of tears, goosebumps, and deep
reflection. Kady's story shares a connection to some of my
own struggles and inspired me to discover and embrace my
strength and what is possible for me."

-Courtney Bondy, Intuitive Yoga Coach

"From the moment I first started reading *Home of the
Soul*, I was hooked. This book took me on a journey that
connected to my soul. From goosebumps to my eyes welling
up with tears. I loved how this journey led to a deeper sense of
purpose and awareness, waiting to become free. A must read!"

-Alysha McLean, Master Business Coach

"When I think of Kady and her book, I think of true grit. . . . Her story is easy to read and relatable to everyone who reads it. . . . Her writing makes you feel you would like to spend time with her and just listen. I am honoured to have had the opportunity to be a part of her journey."
-Judith S. Royle, B.A., M.Ed., M.NLP., MTLT, MCHt,
Master Reiki Teacher

"The way *Home of the Soul* had the ability to draw me in was magical. From the first chapter I was hooked and couldn't wait to tell the story to my family; we sat up for hours by the fireplace with goosebumps as I recalled her journey and how it relates so much to my own experiences. I am a super fan of this book!"
-Sasha Rose, GBR author and hospitality entrepreneur

HOME OF THE SOUL

A TRUE TALE OF MYSTIC ENCOUNTERS THAT AWAKENED MY SPIRIT

KADY ROMAGNUOLO

Published in Canada for Global Distribution by Golden Brick Road Publishing House Inc. Printed in North America.

ISBN: 9781988736228

Author: info@kadymindsetcoach.com

Media: hello@gbrph.ca

Book orders: orders@gbrph.ca

Table of Contents

TO THE READER:

One's personal spiritual experience is made up of interpretations of complex feelings, personal beliefs, and intuitive nuances. This book is an expression of those experiences through memories, internal dialog, and curiosity; a portrayal of thought. A memory is a unique imprint within the mind of who is experiencing it. In each instance a memory may waver in detail from person to person due to the emotional state or previous life experience that one has had. Therefore, memories can often be unreliable or inaccurate and, as such, this book should be read as a story. A story that tells the deep emotional and spiritual connection that was felt by one, but may not have been felt by another. A metaphorical depiction of events. The perspective written here should in no way be taken as infallible truth in regard to a possible death, crime, or malicious act.

INTRODUCTION

Home of the Soul gives the reader a glimpse into the world of unknown energy, spiritual gateways, and how the lives of our ancestors are telling a story that is still unfolding here and now. Have you ever felt lost or unable to understand why your life has seemed to go off course? Perhaps there is a higher meaning behind it? Trusting that all things happen for a reason can be a hard pill to swallow. Being thrown off course from a plan built on hard work and dedication into chaos, trauma, and pain sent me spiraling into deep despair. This story has a lot more to it than what you will read here. There are many facets to this tale. Some are so strange that the dots are still connecting as more information comes to light. As I questioned my own sanity and existence in this world this book was written as a starting point to learn the truth. A way to navigate a web of repressed memories and the blossoming of gifts that I had been hiding out of fear of judgement. I learned that there is no such thing as a coincidence and that signs are everywhere to guide your life. If you're open to embracing these breadcrumbs along your path, there is hope in the midst of your hardest challenges.

The Seed of Life image on this book cover is a sacred geometry symbol known to many cultures, religions, and philosophers. Made up of seven intertwined circles, it symbolizes all of creation and the mystery that our existence holds. As each circle moves to the next this flow represents how events are intertwined and ever expanding in connection with each other. Much like the dots of a storyline aligning to reveal the conclusion.

I had felt a major shift coming within my own life for a number of years leading up to this book. I had been connecting with something not of this world for my entire life and unknowingly drawing in spiritual encounters. In these encounters I learned who I truly was. I had seen how things go off course and their reason, and how the hardest challenges that one can experience can suddenly lead to the most beautiful healing and purpose in life. I now know it's important to let go of how I thought my life should be in order to allow it to turn into more than I could have ever imagined. As you take this journey with me, I hope you travel deep into the space where your soul may be waiting. Expose the shadows, for the dark things we hide will only be transformed to light when we accept that they are there. Embrace the signs, and allow your heart to be guided by an open mind. Are you willing?

Chapter One

UNKNOWN ENERGY

"two complimentary halves"

When I look back at my life, it's now clear to see how all the trauma, depression, and hardships were building up to something. Steve Jobs said, *"You can't connect the dots looking forward; you can only connect them looking backwards."* I've hung onto those words like they were life or death. Those words got me out of bed, kept me from going bankrupt, showed me my true gifts, and ultimately saved my life.

In order to understand the present, it's important to remember the past. Not just the early years of one's life, but also our ancestors. The year 2016 marked the start of the worst three years of my life. Yet to most, I had a life that dreams were made of—beautiful waterfront home, a wonderful husband, and a thriving career. These years, however, would change who I was forever. As I look back now, I realize that I had been holding back who I am and what I knew to be true my entire life. I was filled with secrets that tore at the fabric of my very being. I lived in conflict and chaos, not through unfortunate luck but because of unconscious blocks and repressed memories. I now believe that things happen for a reason, but when everything begins to slowly fall apart and seemingly every piece of you is challenged to the core, it doesn't feel like there would be a reason. These years shook my beliefs and sent my thoughts into utter confusion.

I've always been a dreamer. Believing that there was a grand design for my life, that something special was just around the corner. In 2006 I met Rob, my husband; he was quiet, thoughtful, and seemed to fall out of the sky at the perfect time. I was in my first year of Fashion Design at The International Academy of Design and Technology in Toronto. It was a very isolating experience for me. I had moved across the country on my own at age nineteen with very little resources and no plan, but being a dreamer, I believed that something special was always just around the corner. One year in and I was struggling emotionally, living on my own in a tiny bachelor apartment (where my stove was in the closet), and eating mostly pancakes to survive. It took me eight months of working odd jobs between classes before I could afford to buy a computer and connect with the outside world. I remember going online for the first time and seeing a scrolling banner ad on the side of my screen that caught my eye. It was someone I knew—a familiar face! I was so excited I clicked on the picture not even pausing to see what it was for. It took me to a dating website. It turns out that the person I knew from back home in Alberta had a dating profile and the site was using their photo in an ad. I laughed and thought, *who uses online dating?* Remember, this was well before the popular dating apps of today; it wasn't very common and was considered taboo to some. So, I clicked to send my friend a message, totally intending to poke fun at them. A pop up came on the screen that said: *Sign up to view this profile, it's free! Why not?* I hit start, but there was one problem, I didn't actually want to look for someone to date. I was just bored and craved human interaction. So, I filled in my profile with as many details that I could think of aiming to repel a person looking on a casual dating site. My description had phrases like: looking for marriage and serious long-term relationships only. The key I figured was to have no picture. I thought I would just be skipped over by anyone on the site. Afterall, who is attracted to someone that is giving no information about themselves, but expecting a long-term committed relationship? I thought it was fool proof! As I started to scroll through the pictures in my boredom, one suddenly jumped off the screen at me! There he was, Robert; tall, dark, and handsome. With a slight eye roll I thought to myself, *this guy is a ladies man*. Curious, I scrolled down to see what his bio said. To my surprise it was nearly identical to mine. In that moment, without thinking further ahead, I clicked the little icon on the screen that said: *Send Robert a smile.* Remember, I had crafted a profile that no one could find interesting, without a glamorized selfie or unrealistic perfect pose, no hobbies, talents, or career listed. A blank avatar that had a serious, no nonsense tone. How could it matter if I sent an anonymous little smile? This was my first lesson in energy. The energy that attracts people together through vibration, alignment, and destiny.

The next day I turned on the computer and I had a message. Robert was apparently curious about me. *But why?* My profile was not intriguing, and it couldn't be my picture, I hadn't given one. I responded, again, more curious than anything. We started talking and over the next few weeks I was blown away by how amazing this guy was, but I was also slightly skeptical on why he chose to message me. Finally, I decided to ask, "What made you respond to a profile of someone that said they were looking for marriage and gave no information or picture of themselves?"

His answer was soft, yet concise, "Because you were looking for what I was looking for and everyone with a picture was not showing the real version of themselves anyways." Our connection was immediately strong, but I wouldn't really understand how deep it went until years later.

Four years later Rob and I had been looking for a parcel of land to build our dream home on. Newlywed, we had been searching for a year, but so far nothing felt right. We had a specific vision for what we wanted and somehow that vision seemed to be shared from the moment we met. We imagined a country setting with several acres, and a long driveway winding through a forest that led to a clearing where our home would sit overlooking a lake with no neighbors in sight. The home would be rustic and warm with wood accents and antique details. The land was always what was calling to us more than the house we would build. A specific setting that was vivid and alive in our minds, compromise was not an option.

One day we took a drive out to see a few properties that were for sale about an hour farther than we had previously considered. The whole drive there we said "we're just looking, it's too far. It's good to know all our options." Upon arriving at the three lots that were for sale, we immediately knew they were not right before even getting out of the car. Discouraged, Rob turned the car toward the route home, but I suddenly thought, why not drive down the road a bit further. *Let's just see what this area is like. We've never been here before.* We crossed a narrow bridge that led over a stream and the car came to a stop. "What's down there?" Rob said pointing past me out the window. As I turned my head to see what he was pointing at, my heart started to beat faster. There on the other side of the bridge was a long winding driveway through a dense forest. One so long that we couldn't see where it led to. We could hear water. *What was down there?* I thought to myself, completely consumed in that moment with the enchanting setting. Our energy shifted. Something was drawing our attention here.

We drove home in excitement that day. Neither of us knew why. This property was not for sale. We had no idea what was even back there, nor did we know if there was water through the trees. Something, a gut feeling, told me to investigate. Back at home I quickly got online and looked up the address on a satellite map.

"Rob, come here!" I shouted to him from the living room.

"What, what is it?!" He replied, rushing into the room. I turned the screen towards him and watched his eyes light up. The long winding driveway of this property led to a clearing in the forest with a rustic log home that was overlooking a large lake. No neighbors in sight. It was magical, exactly what we had envisioned; I still recall the feeling that surged through my body in that instant. The excitement however, quickly turned to doubt. This property was not for sale, the home looked massive from the overview image, and it had a lot more land than we had been looking for. Surely, we could not afford this home, even if it were for sale.

I had always believed though that something special was just around the corner and maybe this was it! It took me a while to locate the owner, but once we connected he said, "Yes, we are interested in selling."

One obstacle down. "What price are you looking for?" I asked the man. His reply was three times our budget. Heart-broken, but not surprised, I thanked him and hung up the phone. This was a big second obstacle, and my second lesson in energy. The energy that draws you closer to your life's purpose before you even know what it is. In the eight months following that conversation somehow every financial, personal, and physical obstacle that stood in the path of us and this home were cleared; options and resources presented along our way in perfect sequence. Nearly a year later we were there. Living in our dream home.

It was surreal, the house was five times larger than we needed for just the two of us and we joked about living in only the south wing. The massive log beams soared over twenty feet high to the peak of the roof and the entire main level had floor to ceiling windows that flooded the space with warm sunlight and an expansive view of the water. Sitting up on a hill overlooking the large private lake that we partially owned, the setting was enchanting. A once in a lifetime opportunity. On the surface everyone thought, wow you're so lucky to own such a place at only twenty-five years old. In reality though, neither of us had steady work, we had zero in the bank and ten thousand owing on credit, plus a much larger mortgage than we had ever intended. It was a huge leap of faith. One that I just knew we were drawn to for a reason. A few days after moving in, we immediately started to feel the pressure. Real life and the reality of bills set in. But remember, I was a dreamer and thought that something special was always just around the corner. As I look back this was my third lesson in energy before I knew what I was experiencing. The energy that draws in your present reality; one that attracts into your life exactly what you need in order to heal, but first for you to experience it as raw and very real emotion.

I had been working as a REALTOR® in our previous town for three years and was gaining momentum, but challenges arose with switching areas, starting from scratch, and adding a lot to my plate with this large home. We needed a steady income, and a lot of it for this dream to float. I had sold this idea to my husband and our families, and built up the promise that I was about to thrive in my business and that there was so much I could do with this house. It was decided that it would be a good idea for me to join an established real estate team and gain some stability. I say "it was decided" because I protested the thought of joining a team since the moment I got my license. The thought made me cringe, which made the decision really hard to accept. I had avoided the idea for the last three years! I didn't, however, connect the dots on what those feelings were until many years later. At the time, my reasoning was that I didn't want to work under someone else's direction—I was too independent for that. Looking back, it was the fear of me not being good enough that silently reared its ugly head whenever I thought of joining a team. So, the easiest thing to do to avoid the possibility of working with others where my ability could potentially be compared with someone else's, *not join a team*. That way I had control and I couldn't experience not being good enough. Although the truth was, deep down I already believed that lie and for far longer than the initial suggestion of joining a team. It started many years prior. "*You can't connect the dots looking forward; you can only connect them looking backwards.*" I had many more dots to appear on my timeline before the connections would truly come to light.

Chapter Two

TRUST YOUR GUT

"the grand design"

I began looking for a suitable position on a real estate team. As I picked up the phone to respond to an advertisement one day, I had a horrible feeling in the pit of my stomach. Nerves, I thought. Taking direction from someone else and not having full say over my day-to-day were things I did not want to do, but the tradeoff meant a stable income. I worried that joining a team would take away from the growth of my own brand, and leave me with no recognition to build on. I pushed that nervous feeling aside and made the call. It was a simple interview process; I had a competent skill level that any team leader would find an asset, so they offered me the position. The day I was told "congratulations you've got the position!" my heart sank. Was the tradeoff bigger than I knew? Was this the right decision? Why did I have this horrible sinking feeling in the pit of my stomach?

The position was an incredible amount of work. I was driving two to five hours a day taking on tasks that were completely outside of the job description and not making much more money than previously. Everyday I felt exhausted, worn out, and taken advantage of, yet, I never spoke up or said no to the additional duties. Everyday I would tell myself that I was doing this for a reason; we were gaining the home of our dreams, building a future, and someday we would retire and have a bed-and-breakfast there. It kept me going. Every time someone asked me to take on a few more duties, help out a little more, I got that same sinking feeling that I felt the day I was hired. Again, I pushed it away and told myself I was doing this for a reason.

Have you ever felt stuck in a role you never expected yourself to be in? Have you ever looked back and asked yourself, *how did I get here?* It was a blur for me, almost as if I woke up one day and didn't recognize myself. I was suddenly someone who had no boundaries; overworked, underpaid, and unappreciated. Just to live in a beautiful home. A home that I now could no longer enjoy because there wasn't enough free time to spend there. I was too busy working.

This trap seems to be common for so many in our society. Everywhere you look someone is rushing to get to the next place, grumpy because they didn't get enough sleep, or too stressed to enjoy their vacation because they paid for it on credit and that bill will take them years to pay off, if ever. Why do we do this to ourselves? In my case, there was a void to be filled; a part of me that never felt safe and secure as a child. I was unconsciously trying to create a stable, warm, loving home for myself, but my version of it was skewed and attached to money and recognition. Two areas that, again, had been lacking in my childhood.

Growing up in my household was a very scary place. My experience with a miserable father, who most days seemed to hate his life, left a big impression on me. I don't remember spending much time together as a family. I was too afraid to say or do something wrong. Fantasies of moving and starting a fresh life far away from the complexities of my family filled my head. Dad would come home from work so miserable about his day that he needed to be left alone for hours before you could approach him or even speak. When it appeared to be safe to talk, I had to be very careful about which tone I used, even for the slightest of phrases; I didn't want to be accused of talking back. I learned early on that it was dangerous to have an opposing opinion. Most days, the fear of speaking up was enough to keep me in line. It may not have been obvious, but I was a very stressed out kid, I adapted early on to hide it well. A natural instinct for my self-preservation. I had, however, developed Irritable Bowel Syndrome at a young age and encountered countless doctor's appointments;

stress was the only conclusion that the doctors would ever give. We did the food journals, allergy testing, and anything else they could think of. All inconclusive. Ultimately, it only ever boiled down to what I was thinking and feeling when my stomach was causing me excruciating pain. My flare ups were onset in times where I was fearful. By age twelve I would close my eyes and pray as hard as I could that I would not wake up in the morning. I didn't want to face another day, but had been raised with religious values so taking my own life was not an option. I remember crying myself to sleep and wondering why God would rather me suffer each day and live in such a controlling and manipulative environment. As I think back now, it really did save my life; believing that there would be a consequence to killing myself, that I would go to Hell, prevented me from taking action.

Now as an adult I had moved away from home, started a life of my own and was drawn in by the idea that I could have a dream life, a warm and loving home. I was so close I could touch it. This house, for me, represented love, appreciation, recognition, and a new life the instant I was in its presence. This house spoke to my heart from the moment I laid eyes on her. The problem was I wasn't listening to my guidance system, the one that gave me a pit in my stomach when I was veering off course.

> *"Not only does the thought you are choosing right now attract the next thought, and the next, and so on—it also provides the basis of your alignment with your inner being."* -Abraham Hicks

I read this phrase years later, after accepting the position on the real estate team, as I attempted to connect the dots of my life and understand who I truly was. What was my inner being? Did I even have one? At first I did my best to fit in on the team, follow directions, and be helpful. That eventually led me to doing the work that no one else would. Dealing with the unruly clients that were unappreciative, running around performing errands that had nothing to do with my job title, and having my pay diminished unfairly to compensate for the actions of another team member. I never spoke up to say that I felt used. Instead, I pushed my feelings down and let them take advantage of my hard work. It was an all too familiar feeling from my childhood. Stay quiet and do as you're told to stay safe. Here, safety translated into keeping my job. Slowly, yet surely, like the Titanic hitting an iceberg, I had been leading my life towards the emotional destruction that would take place a few years later. Each day that I remained complacent to a role conflicted with my personal values and out of alignment with my truest self, I attracted more negative experiences and thoughts. The more I took on, the less I was appreciated, and the more my thoughts grew of low self-worth. This pull of negative feelings festered and grew. The more I rationalized the need to pay the bills with money from a job I hated and that treated me poorly, the worse my financial state got. I remember thinking, *I deserve better than this*, but that thought instantly brought up all the old feelings from my childhood. Memories that were terrifying and just like that, I felt like the little girl again who couldn't do anything right, who hid her self-doubt to stay safe. I had worked so hard to get to where I was, out of the low-income neighborhood I was raised in, and away from the violence of my childhood. How had I allowed myself to lose sight of my personal values and independence, all just for money? I struggled to remember why I was pushing so hard to make this job work. Was this house really worth it?

There are times in life where you'll get a nudge towards what could be. A glimpse of what is possible for your life. This happens for everyone. The tricky part is getting good at saying yes; overcoming the fear of the unknown and the trap of what society conditions us to believe we are. It's the exciting opportunity that you turn down because you think it's not the right time. The relationship that seems too good to be true. The trip you want to take, but are too worried about how your family will cope while you're away. What if we all said yes a little more to the things we truly wanted? What if your internal guidance system was unique and only you knew how to navigate it? What if I had listened to my gut feeling that said I was taking a job that didn't feel right for me? It would take me a few more years to gain the courage to look inside myself for what I wanted.

We attract into our lives the things we need to heal, I believe this wholeheartedly. I still needed to heal the part of me that craved recognition for my work, to feel good enough to deserve a loving and happy home. In order to heal those parts of me, I needed to face where they came from and be aware that they still existed; when I moved away, those feelings were packed unknowingly beside my treasured belongings and hitched a ride to the next location. For healing to happen, I needed to experience the extreme contrast of feeling completely unappreciated for me to realize my desire to feel loved, so that I could take another perspective and make a change. That strong pull that I felt leading me to this home, perhaps, had more to it than I thought.

Confused and conflicted with where I now found myself in life, I questioned my ability to make decisions. At this point I was secretly developing a lot of anxiety; worried about everything I did throughout the day; replaying conversations on a loop assessing what I should have said differently. It was a painful existence, but I told no one. I felt that if I did I would lose my job because it relied on me being a good negotiator. Who would want to hire an agent to sell their home in one of the most competitive markets in the country that was afraid to talk to people? Instead I put on a fake smile, pretended to be confident, and then cried in my car on the way home most days. It was too much to bear. I felt like I was losing more of myself each day, but couldn't understand it because I had dreamt my entire life of being a real estate agent. I had always loved the idea of showing homes, writing contracts, and contributing to the stability of someone's financial future. Helping people build their own happy home. I was proud to be a homeowner and believed that everyone should be able to feel that pride.

I decided to try something new and look for a business coach or mentor to help me feel more confident and assertive in my daily tasks, but I became too worried about admitting that I felt like an insecure mess to someone who worked in my industry. Fear of judgement took over and I again pushed my anxious feelings down, I kept working, but felt like a complete failure.

"Until you make the unconscious conscious, it will direct your life and you will call it fate"
-Carl Jung

I thought I was destined to become my parents; spend my life working in a thankless position that stole a little more of my soul each day. My anxiety ruled my decisions. Why hadn't I trusted my gut, my internal guidance system? That sharp feeling I felt initially when I knew that this position wasn't for me, not what my heart wanted. Have you ever thought about what causes that gut feeling? How does your internal guidance system work?

In my very early childhood before the structure of my household and it's religion took hold, nothing could stop me. I was wild and unreserved, free. Now I could only grab a brief glimpse of that little girl in fleeting moments before the buzz in my chest took over and I was unsure of myself again. The buzz of my heartbeat felt like a rapid, constant hum; my entire body convulsing quickly on the inside, but no one else could see it. My experience of anxiety and panic attacks. As I veered further and further off course from who I naturally was, my body responded in kind; my guidance system screamed, *you're going the wrong way!* I obviously wasn't paying attention.

I remember learning scripting for sales calls, the dialog seemed so cold and insincere. I had a lot of trouble even trying to practice the words, they felt very unnatural and forced. Slowly I was adapting to the ways of someone else and it never felt right. I was always hard on myself, thinking I just wasn't cut out for this work, but the thought of quitting the business also made me sad to my core. I couldn't understand my confliction of why my dreams of being successful were tied to an industry in which I found so challenging to be myself. There had to be a reason.

* * *

The home needed a fair bit of work to bring it to its full beauty, the image we envisioned, so we had to keep working our grueling schedules to achieve our goal. Every dollar we made went back into our lake house. Rob worked in construction and operated a small renovation company, so he took our house project on himself. He spent his days driving two hours one way to his job sites in the city, working a full day, then spending hours late into the evening bringing our vision to light. Every project was a struggle. We'd take one step forward then two steps back. The original rustic hardwood floors were all refinished in a beautiful glass-like finish, the natural light sparkled across its surface. I remember waking up the very next morning after we completed the floors, admiring the new space for the first time. Walking into the kitchen my heart stopped. The floor was ruined! The hardwood that had stretched across the room and into the kitchen was warped and uneven. Overnight the fridge had malfunctioned and poured water all over the freshly finished surface. This was one of many setbacks. It started to feel like we were not meant to live here in peace; life was destined to be a struggle.

Chapter Three

WAITING TO LIVE

"the enchanted forest"

When you believe that you are sacrificing for a reason, a demanding schedule, little sleep, and limited personal time seem acceptable. "At least you have your health," was commonly said to Rob and me. True, until suddenly we didn't. Stress kills. I had never really thought about it. When young, life is wide open, ready for the taking. I'd already experienced how stress in my childhood gave me excruciating stomach pain, but that wasn't serious, not life threatening. As we continued to swim through the deep waters of financial strain and limited sleep, it seemed to be catching up with us. At first, Rob started complaining of minor aches and pains; he had a physical job and was working around the clock so we didn't think much of it. It was logical that his body would grow tired of the constant strain. But we had an end game, this was only temporary and he would then regain a more balanced life once we completed the work. Do not wait to live—words I do not say lightly.

Rob was getting weaker and weaker and you could see the strain in his face; his eyes were dark and his skin pale; he started becoming too weak to make it into work. At first I thought, *okay he needs a break to regain his strength, then get back to it.* Then the more specific symptoms started; intense pain in his right shoulder that nearly immobilized his whole right side. Most days he could barely lift his head and I could hardly get a word out of him. He wasn't sleeping or eating. The doctors were not finding anything, but could see that it was getting serious. "Are you depressed, young man?" a Doctor asked in one of our visits. Hardly making eye contact, Rob shrugged his shoulders with a short small movement. That was a yes. I knew things had been hard, but was the stress actually taking away his ability to move? Physically restricting him to be bedridden at only thirty years old? It was emotional for me to watch and I grew tired of doctor visits that gave us no answers. The weeks went on and as we sat in another cold, sterile, white room waiting for a specialist to enter, I could feel my anxiety rising. I couldn't watch him deteriorate like this; we had to get some answers today. "You seem to have a lot of inflammation in your joints for a man of your age. Can you think of anything that you might have recently changed in your lifestyle that could be contributing to this?" the specialist asked, with a strange tension in his voice. He then stepped directly in between where I was sitting and where Rob was on the exam table, blocking my line of sight to him and asked again. It was like a scene from a dramatic court case where the prosecutor places themselves in front of the perpetrator while they ask the victim to tell the truth despite the accused sitting in the room listening to them. I was confused and now unable to read their body language or gain eye contact between them. What was going on here? Did I miss something in all of this? The doctor turned to me, "Can I ask you to please leave the room, ma'am." He wasn't really asking . . . as his eyes stared deep into mine. I got up and walked out of the room with a horrible feeling in the pit of my stomach. A few minutes later the doctor brought me back in. My emotions were now on high alert. What had they been talking about?

"It appears that you may have a rare form of Rheumatoid Arthritis, which is uncommon for your age or possibly an immune disorder. I suggest we try a steroid injection to help with your pain," the doctor said and turned to write on his notepad.

"What?!" I bursted out. "That's it? What is the treatment, there must be a more specific diagnosis? This doesn't make any sense." My eyes filled with tears and I could feel the desperation in my voice.

"There's not much more we can do at this point. Let's see how the next few weeks go," he replied.

I was angry, confused, and scared. Did he not understand what it was like to watch someone you love disintegrating before your eyes. He was becoming a shell of the man I once knew, withdrawn and isolated. We got in the car to drive home and I turned to Rob and asked, "What happened in that room after I left?"

"They just asked me a few more questions," he replied.

"What questions?" I asked.

"They were trying to understand my emotional state. Why was I so quiet and if I had been involved in something that would have been contributing to my sudden symptoms," he said.

"Well what did you tell them?!" I asked. Didn't they understand that I was just as confused about what was going on as them? They seemed to think that there was something he was not telling them and that's why they asked me to leave to give him privacy to disclose any important information.

"I told them I didn't know," Rob replied.

I was feeling completely alone. There was still a lot of work to do on the house, but we couldn't afford to hire contractors to do the work and Rob was in no shape to try. I was silently hating myself for feeling a connection to this home to begin with; for encouraging us to get into this. It was clearly too much for him. I started to blame the house. The house is making him sick. Months went by with no improvement. I was terrified that his depression was taking over. He'd lay in bed unable to move with flu-like symptoms. Why was I fine? I wasn't getting sick yet felt just as much pressure, especially now that our income was reduced. Again, my thoughts went to the house. *Why are you doing this to him?!* The voice inside my head screamed. I started to fantasize about getting him out of there. If I could only pick him up and get him out of that house maybe he would improve. It made no sense, I had no real reason to logically think the house was draining him of energy and life, but it felt like that was the only explanation.

One day I came home from work and Rob was up out of bed! He was walking around outside, in the forest. I could see a slight improvement within him. It was like my vision of him getting out of the house and being revitalized was unfolding before my eyes. I had a moment of hope. The days after he continued to improve. He was spending more time outside and regaining strength. A short time later he returned to work and also picked up where he had left off on the house. Most people assumed he just needed a break, that that was enough to refuel his energy and he was back to his old self. The inflammation causing his mobility constraints and debilitating pain had suddenly vanished. I believed it was something more, but kept it to myself. *Had the forest healed him?* Was my first thought. What a strange idea, even I felt a little crazy to think about it. Nonsense. We were moving forward again, everything would be okay, or so I thought.

There was a loud bang and I heard footsteps shuffling in quickly. I was in the kitchen cleaning up from dinner, Rob had been working late outside on the garage. He was finishing the new siding. I heard the shower turn on and so I continued what I was doing. A short time later it was quiet so I went up to see why he hadn't come back downstairs. He was lying in bed, visibly in pain. "What's going on?" I asked. No reply. The silence scared me; an instant reminder of the year previous when he had fallen into a deep depression. I noticed he had elevated his foot underneath the covers so I pulled them back to see. His leg was propped up on the pillow and wrapped tight with a tensor bandage. "What happened?" I asked.

"I think I broke my ankle," he finally replied in a sharp tone. "I fell off the roof of the garage."

"What?! How did you get back here and up the stairs?" I asked in shock. The garage was a lengthy walk from the house, up the driveway towards the road. Somehow he had managed to get himself back to the house, cleaned up, and in bed. At the emergency room the x-rays confirmed he had broken his ankle and would now need to be off work again for six to eight weeks.

I wondered how he had taken such a serious fall and had the ability to walk all that way back to the house and not cause further damage to his leg. It was a two story building and he had fallen from the top. A twenty foot drop. The garage was tucked away in the forest off a side trail from the driveway, a beautiful setting of hundred-year old trees that towered over the landscape. In just the right lighting it was a magical spot. The canopy of the tree tops spread wide across the skyline sheltering the garage from sight. *Had something in the forest protected him? Gave him strength to get back to the house?* Again, I felt crazy for even thinking about it, but couldn't help my curiosity.

The injury meant he would be stuck in the house (again) for much of each day. I was worried that he would fall back into the place he was in where sadness and pain took over. Each day I could see it creeping closer. *I need to get him out of here,* I thought to myself. We had been planning a trip to Mexico before the fall. We needed a break to reconnect, and the date was fast approaching. How could he go on this trip with a broken ankle though? I trusted my gut and insisted we still go. The doctors told him it should be okay and that perhaps it would do him good to get out of the house and move. Exactly, my thoughts, too. We agreed to go on the trip. It went well and took our minds off the daily stress and pressure of finishing the house.

Upon arriving home from our vacation something felt off. The energy was heavy in the air the moment we stepped in. I could feel it, but was it just me? Maybe it was just the weight of getting back to reality? I remember having the sudden feeling of being punished for spending some money on us instead of improving the home. Like the house had feelings of its own and it was upset with us for leaving her alone for a week with a stranger that was house sitting. What was this strange emotional connection I had to this house? I was fixated on what I felt it needed to feel loved and appreciated. Was that just me projecting my own thoughts and feelings, ones I still needed to heal from as a child, onto my current situation? Rob apparently felt it too and had had enough. He immediately turned to me and without hesitation or discussion said "we're selling this house," and walked away.

I was in shock. How could he be so cold? I felt the tension too, but I never thought we would ever consider selling the house. We had put our heart and soul into getting here, spent years on the renovations, worked thankless jobs and sacrificed our time, energy, health, and money. We had sold our investments and borrowed from family. How could he ask me to do this? Quietly, to myself the next day, I sat and thought about what it would really mean to sell the house. Would it mean that I could quit my job with the team I was on and get back to my initial goal of having my own successful real estate business? Could we eliminate the stress of trying to keep up the appearance that everything was okay? Could Rob stop working himself to death? I realized that it was for the best, but with tears in my eyes felt deep sadness. *How could my feelings have been so wrong about this house?* I thought it was meant for us. We had moved mountains to get here. All for what? To give up?

There was still a lot of work to do to get the house in prime selling condition. At least we could potentially make some money off our years of investment. We sat down and developed a plan; what had to be done, what it would cost, and how long it would take. Ultimately, we needed another year to complete the work and have enough money to do it. So, we put our heads down again and focused on getting through the next year. Time moved in slow motion at this point. I continued working in a position that sucked the life out of me, and it wasn't for the *good* reasons of living in our dream home anymore, but to fund being able to sell her. It was painful for me to think about, so I didn't. The plan was to go back to our original plan and find a small piece of land to build on. The idea was still calling to us both, so maybe we were just meant for somewhere else; a redirection? I tried to see the positive, but just felt lost and confused—broken about our dreams.

We were getting close to listing the house for sale. The finishing touches were almost done and the property was now stunning. Completely revived to its full glory. The grounds were perfectly landscaped with cobblestone pathways and outdoor gathering areas with a stone fireplace overlooking the lake. Trails were groomed to walk the forest and a fountain installed that gave way to the gentle sound of trickling water. Inside, the original character and warmth of the log was maintained and revitalized with an infusion of modern design. It was perfect, just as we had imagined it. A space created with love and endurance. There was a sense of relief in the air. Opportunity to start fresh with more equity in hand and the possibility of new energy in a different space; one that didn't hold the memories of pain and depression.

We had a lot of interest as soon as our house hit the market; it was great timing, a seller's market, and prices were strong. Homes were being sold in multiple offers and well over the asking price. Finally, maybe, our luck had shifted. Maybe this was the reason we were here. A stepping stone to start off in a good financial position and for me to leave my current job with loads of experience and open my own real estate brokerage. I was excited again for the first time in years. An offer came in immediately. This was a great sign. As the conversation started with the other agent to adjust a few details, suddenly the buyer decided it wasn't for them. The house was exactly what they were looking for, but for an unknown reason they backed away from the offer. *Strange, but that's okay,* I thought. We had just listed. Over the next year the same pattern repeated—over and over again. A buyer would make an offer then change their mind, there was never a reason; no failed home inspection or exact reason provided as to why the change of heart. Often the feedback I received was: "The house is stunning, absolutely a dream property, but it's just not for us. It's a great price so you'll have no trouble selling it." Repeatedly, everyone around us was confused at all the failed offers. The trouble was, we had borrowed money from everywhere we could to make the final stretch to finish the renovations while the market was strong. We had also found a smaller parcel of land that was waiting for us when we sold the house. It took a great deal of maneuvering financially to buy it while the house was still for sale, but somehow we made it work. At this point we were overextended and working just as hard as ever to maintain multiple property payments. It was not a long term plan, we thought the house would sell quickly, but something was holding us back.

Year two of the house for sale felt like a long episode of *The Twilight Zone.* At this point I was making good money within my current position. The thriving real estate market had allowed me to excel at what I was doing and relieve a lot of the financial strain, but each time I sold a home I felt that horrible pit in my stomach. *Why couldn't I sell my own home?* Those same inadequate feelings from my childhood crept back in. Most days I felt like a complete fraud. The most tiresome thing was to keep showing the house; to keep marketing and promoting it over and over again, only to get a buyer then have them back out for no reason. Several times buyers seemed to fall off the face of the earth. Never to give a reason for why the final paperwork was not signed and never to be heard from again. Calls and messages were unanswered as if we were living in a bubble. Trapped. My anxiety was rising and I felt like I couldn't share that with anyone. I didn't want to appear weak in my skill level within my work, and I couldn't risk Rob falling into another depression. Somewhere inside of me I still believed that something special was just around the corner. If we could just hold on.

I was asked to go to a real estate conference that Fall. It was a three day event and the idea of attending with some of the top agents in my field made me want to die. *What if they ask me about the house? Why it hasn't sold yet?* I was embarrassed and constantly avoided the subject. I ended up attending and did my best to portray a confident, put together professional, but I was ready to crack. One of the break out sessions was about our unconscious behaviors and how our emotions, thoughts, and internal self-talk create our life experience. I immediately felt connected to what the trainers were talking about and needed to know more. I signed up for a workshop on the topic that took place after the conference. As I approached one trainer during break, it took everything in me to control my hands from shaking. With tears in my eyes I said, "I'm really struggling with anxiety." That was the first time I had said it outloud. It would start my journey here, to this book, to my gifts.

I embraced the concepts I was learning at the workshop about emotional health, one's unconscious values, and the role we have in choosing our actions—it helped me tremendously. I was thirsty for knowledge and it was feeding a part of my soul that had been neglected for so long. By the end of the day I was certain that there was something I needed to explore and I enrolled in their practitioner training. In the year following I completed all of my certifications in Neuro Linguistic Programming and became certified with the American Board of Hypnotherapy. Perhaps this was the reason for all of the odd deals that fell apart on our home. If the house had sold, I would have left my position on the real estate team and would have never been at that conference. I would not have met the two trainers with whom I immediately felt connected and would not have found the work I do today that fulfills a part of me that I was desperately trying to find. Back to what Steve Jobs said, *"you can't connect the dots looking forward; you can only connect them looking backwards."* I was convinced we were now ready. This was it. What needed to happen before I could cut my emotional tie to the house and she could let us go, but . . . there was more for me to learn there first.

Chapter Four

1338

"the forgotten key"

Has it followed me my entire life? My memories as a child are more vivid than yesterday's. I grew up in a small bungalow that was built by my grandfather. The once small town had been absorbed by the city and disintegrated slowly in crime. It still felt like home to both my parents and we didn't have a lot of money to move to a better area, so they started their family there. Our home had no basement, just two bedrooms and one bathroom for our family of four. I remember the year that mom and dad decided we needed more space, I must have been only four or five years old. The entire home was jacked up and the earth beneath was dug down to create a lower level. The basement was poured, and we suddenly doubled our living space. The thing was we never really finished that level; perhaps it was a matter of finances, or maybe we were so used to living in the smaller square footage that we didn't venture downstairs often. The floor remained concrete and an area rug and large chair were placed down there.

I remember the first time I woke up suddenly in the basement and not my warm bed upstairs in my room. It was pitch black and I was sitting in that large armchair. At first, I was really disoriented. *How did I get down here?* I remember going to bed and falling asleep upstairs in my room. Why was I suddenly sitting in the chair in the basement? How did I get down here in the pitch black? I was in a state of trance; sleepwalking. Have you ever experienced a dream where you felt like the room was not the room you were in? That you felt like you couldn't control your actions, but that you were slightly aware of them? In a fog but unable to control your words or movements? This is what sleepwalking is like for me. I still do this as an adult, but this house, 1338, was where it all started.

I could hear her talking, whispering something in my left ear. It was quiet and not clear enough for me to decipher. As I leaned towards her, my trance-like state loosened and I became aware of where I was. It was pitch black and I was in the basement again. Listening to an old woman who sat next to the large armchair. She was cloaked in black and very still. The first time I saw her I don't recall being afraid. I was curious. She was trying to tell me something, but I couldn't make it out. I'd slowly come to my full awareness of where I was, like swimming through dense murky waters, and would walk back up the stairs, crawl into my bed, and drift back to sleep. This happened often. I remember telling my parents and being told "you leave that alone," in a stern voice. I knew that voice and did not disobey it. Thinking back now as an adult the response was odd. Leave what alone? Did they know something about this?

The weeks passed and my sister started to tell me stories right before bed about the monsters under my bed. We shared a room with a bunk bed, and I was on the lower level. I never understood why she would purposely terrify me right before we'd go to sleep. It made me so angry. She was my older sister, she was supposed to look out for me; protect me. To my surprise years later I discovered the terrifying truth behind her stories.

It had been thirty years since we lived at 1338. I had nearly completely forgotten about the woman I had been trying to communicate with in the basement; chalked it up to a recurring dream and hadn't mentioned it to anyone. I had moved to Toronto fourteen years prior and was back in Calgary to visit my family. The trip was not unusual to any other and as my sister and I sat on the couch that evening, she looked over at me and casually said, "Remember when you used to sit in the basement in the middle of the night?" I was shocked. How did she know this? She continued, "I was so afraid for

you that I had to make up that story about the monsters under your bed to protect you."

"What?!" I gasped, "What do you mean?"

She started to explain, "I would wake up in the middle of the night and have a feeling that you were downstairs. Ever since we raised the house and dug the basement you were drawn to it. I would find you sitting in the large armchair in the dark, talking to someone."

"What do you mean talking to someone?" I asked, knowing the answer, but probing her for more information.

She continued, "The woman sitting beside you. She was in a rocking chair and sometimes singing to you. I would stand at the top of the stairs and call out to you, but you wouldn't respond." I was completely shocked. This was a memory that we shared. The same image, the same occurrence. It was not a dream of mine. I had been visiting with something, or someone, in the basement.

"I was trying to get you to stop," my sister said, "The only way I could think of was to tell you there were monsters under your bed." It all made perfect sense, I realized.

The terrifying stories that I would be grabbed and dragged by my ankles under the bed to be eaten alive had a purpose. She was my older sister that was trying to protect me, the only way she knew how to, as a young child herself. Her hope was that I would be too scared to get out of bed. I turned to her and asked, "So, did it work?"

"Yes," she replied, "but only for a short while. The woman started coming up to our bedroom instead." As I recalled those nights again in my mind, I saw the image of the dark shadowed woman standing at our bedroom door; remembering clearly now, as a child I would rub my eyes to clear my vision, but the image wouldn't fade. The dark shadowed woman would stand there silently staring at us. I used to close my eyes so tightly, sure that if I couldn't see her then she was

not there. My sister had the same memory. She too saw the dark shadowed woman standing in the door frame. Soon after we moved, and the woman didn't follow, but something else did—my sleepwalking.

What had we experienced as children in that home? How did we have the same memory, but never talked about it? That night we talked about many of the other things we remembered in that home; the large canvas picture that fell from the wall right on top of me; the plastic ball that bounced down the hall with no one in sight; the faint sounds of music that no one but us could hear. I did a lot of strange things in my sleep during this period and no one seemed to think much of it. Now as an adult, I wondered if I had been experiencing spirits that were trying to communicate with me before I even knew what spirits were?

Other memories started to come back; I clearly remember my father who was very religious at the time constantly saying protection prayers, but they scared me. He would rebuke the Devil and call in Archangels to surround our home. I had totally repressed these memories until now. It began to feel like he knew something more than we did, like he had believed that he was trying to protect us from something sinister.

My sleep continued to be erratic in the next house. We had moved into a newly built home and I had a room of my own and my sister slept downstairs. I had always seemed to be drawn down to her room. In the morning she would tell me how I was hovering over her bed again in the night, sleepwalking. She would guide me back to my room. Eventually the events started to escalate and became dangerous for me. I started trying to leave the home out the front door. My parents must have been terrified that I would end up wandering into the street, so they placed a latch at the top on the door where I could not reach it. That's when I remember the recurring night terrors starting and the insistence that my bed-

room door be closed when I slept. I have always been afraid of sleeping with the door open and it now made sense after recalling the image of the shadowed woman standing in my door frame. Unconsciously, I was afraid of her returning in my sleep.

I wasn't certain what I believed now; had I been experiencing something that couldn't be explained with common logic? Before Rob and I were about to move in together to my small apartment in Toronto, I had never discussed my sleepwalking or odd occurrences from my childhood with him. Living alone for a while at that point, I wasn't sure if I was still sleepwalking. One day he turned to me and said, "You need to move those large scissors you have in your bedside table before I move in." Confused, I asked "why?" I had been attending Fashion Design School at the time and lived alone in the downtown core in a building that had no security; I slept with my large fabric shears in my nightstand. My logic was that if there was an intruder I would reach for my shears. It gave me some sort of comfort. Rob simply replied "you sleepwalk and do strange movements in your sleep and I'm a bit worried that you may accidentally use those scissors on me in our sleep." I was shocked and horrified. I thought to myself, *I would never!* Then it struck me, I was still walking in my sleep and he knew. I was suddenly embarrassed. What had I been doing in my sleep? Why had I no recollection of it? I removed the scissors from the bedside, agreeing that I didn't need them anymore.

A few years later Rob and I were living in our first home we had purchased together; it was on Cemetery Lane. Others thought it was strange that I felt so at home living beside a large cemetery at the end of the tiny cul-de-sac, but it was peaceful there. I remember walking on the narrow dirt pathways between the headstones and feeling a sense of calm. However, my nightly sleepwalking and talking heightened again in this home. Once, I awoke in the middle of the night, the room was pitch black and I was leaning over the edge of the bed, suspended with my nose pressed against the wall. It was a very awkward position that took a lot of core strength to sustain. Suddenly aware of my position, I moved abruptly and sat up in the bed wondering why I was just doing that; I'm curious now if I was leaning over to hear something, perhaps something from the graveyard on the other side of that wall that my head was pressed against? It was an eerily similar feeling to leaning out of the large armchair in the basement as a child to try and hear the woman's voice all those years ago. Was she back? Here with me? Or was this something else. It didn't end there. Rob would wake me from a delirious state; babbling and asking him incoherent questions with frustration. The feeling was like thinking through mental fog; a blurry sensation. I could tell I was doing this when it was happening, but couldn't stop myself. It was like I was hearing myself speak through a bubble, muffled with words that were out of order. It never made sense. When I came to with more clarity we could never figure out what I was trying to get through with my babble. What were my questions about? Then suddenly one day it changed and I started to make specific hand gestures while asleep. It was focused on Rob and, again, I felt like I couldn't stop myself from doing it.

I finally began to realize why he didn't want those scissors by the bed; I was now waking in mid movement above his chest, suspended over his body as if in a protective stance, but motioning back and forth, feeling afraid of something the moment I would wake. If I had unintentionally had those fabric sheers in my hand out of a state of fear, was it possible that I could have done him harm in my sleep? It was like a recurring dream, but without the dream, just action. I couldn't stop myself from hovering over him each night. All I knew was that it felt like I was protecting him in the immediate moments after I woke.

We had lived together now for over eleven years, while my sleep occurrences continued. Throughout all these years, they always seemed to be focused around Rob. Initially when we had moved into our dream home on the lake we were concerned that I might walk out into the water and drown. My safety had always been a concern in my childhood because of my constant attempts to leave our childhood home in my sleep all those years ago.

One night I suddenly woke up sitting in the familiar suspended position above Rob, he was totally unaware, fast asleep. I abruptly woke him because this time was different, I was terrified because I saw that something was coming down on him and the motion I was doing was trying to frantically save him. *From what, was I dreaming?* "What just happened?" Rob asked.

"I don't know, I can't explain it," I replied, "I think I was dreaming but it felt so real. I thought I saw something coming down on you. I think it was something mechanical, falling." It didn't make sense to either of us. What did mechanical mean and why was this experience so vivid for me this time, unlike the other times? I would get my answer soon enough.

Chapter Five

ASK AND YOU SHALL
RECEIVE

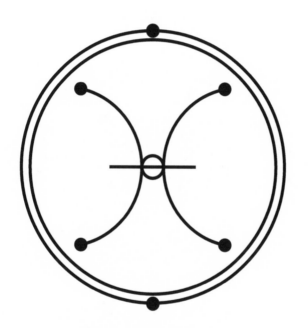

"fantasy and reality"

Just before we decided to sell our dream house, I had developed such a love and connection to the property that in my eyes the structure took form as "She" and I felt close to her. She took on a presence in my life and I found myself speaking softly to her on occasion to comfort and tell her it would all be okay. That we would find a family to love her as much as I did and that I was not abandoning her. Perhaps I was speaking to myself. Trying to reassure myself. I called her Laure. An uncommon name that seemed to roll off my tongue one day. Laure (Loor) is described as someone who is innately optimistic, who loves to sing, and is compassionate. Serious yet majestic. Derived from the more popular name Laurel, like the Laurel Flower, which is symbolic of a marked achievement. In some stories the Laurel Flower has also been given as a token of false pride, as if to mock. The meaning encompassed much of my feelings towards the home's presence and the situation we found ourselves in. I had felt as if we had received a false sense of achievement in this home.

Most nights I toss and turn in my sleep. My anxiety is heightened to the point where I'm waking up in the middle of the night frantic, my heart racing and I'm experiencing the feeling of panic. Jumping out of bed I rush outside into the woods. I'm hearing sounds, cries. *Is this in my head?* I seem to be the only one hearing it. It sounds more like shrieks; high pitched and startling. I wonder if it's the coyotes, or is it something else? My first thought is always to protect; I jump out of bed and rush outside into the brisk, cold, dark night because we have two dogs and they are outside; I'm terrified for them. Every night the same thing happens; I'm barely sleeping, alert, and ready to run as my head is still resting.

I've often wondered if I ever actually sleep. I seem to re-member the hours of each night passing and drifting in and out of dreams that are so vivid that it feels like they are real life. Like I'm in another dimension of space and time. Rob has been curious enough to want to record what happens in the deep hours of the night throughout the house. He thinks it would be good for me to see what I'm doing, maybe make a connection to my movements, but I'm too scared to know. The times that I reach deep sleep feel like time travel, I've been so used to being slightly coherent in my sleep that when I'm fully resting, and not conscious, it's unfamiliar. It feels like I've lost time; like I don't know where I've been.

"*WAKE UP KADY,*" a deep voice bellows within my ears. My eyes are wide open, but when did they open? It was so dark in the room that I didn't know if I was still sleeping. I blinked but felt like I couldn't move. Holding my breath I intently listen to hear who just spoke. The sound was so loud, the tone was deep and unrecognizable. Silence. There was no one there.

A few nights later, Rob and I were getting ready for bed when I suddenly stopped and put my finger over my lips to motion him to be silent. "Do you hear that?" I said.

"Hear what?" he replies, straining his ear towards me.

"That music," I replied. It was as if a full orchestra of instruments were echoing through the forest. I peered out the window into the vastness of the dark treeline wondering where it was coming from.

"I don't hear anything," Rob says, and continues about his business.

What was happening to me? I needed to understand. Why was I so restless and where were these sounds coming from? Were they all in my head?

The nights continued with me roaming the rooms of the house as I walked in my sleep in the deepest hours of the night, as if searching for unconscious answers to a question I hadn't asked. Sleep was when I felt free, yet I couldn't tell when I was sleeping or drifting. Drifting for me is an out-of-body experience; there are times when I feel like I'm there with me in the room, seeing myself but through another's eyes. I feel as though I'm in another time or place. The moments are quick, incoherent, and the feeling is unexplainable, very different from dreaming. These nights I'm uneasy when I wake, unsure of my surroundings or where I am. Do I have a connection with something far greater than I? I had always believed in God and felt that there was a higher power that helped guide my life, but my experience with religion as a child had been controlling and self-serving for the people in charge. There had always been a hint of manipulation and hypocrisy in my household's version, leaving me uncertain and weary of spirituality.

A question unasked will always go unanswered. In my world I felt as though I was drawing in an answer to something big; something greater than I, so who was asking the question? Was I living through another person's eyes in my sleep? Was I looking for an answer to a question that my soul was asking, not my conscious mind? Some people discover in their lifetime that they have a unique ability to make others laugh or are naturally present as leaders in times of struggle. My unique ability was strange and fascinating; scary yet intriguing; evolving yet completely incoherent. Although, I hadn't discovered what it was exactly, what it all meant, or if I was just going crazy.

We attract into our lives the things we need to heal. I had experienced so many traumas already in my life; violence and abuse in my childhood, self-devaluation as I gravitated to jobs that left me feeling undeserving, and a self-imposed isolation out of fear of judgment. I was afraid of what I was doing in my sleep, fearful of the sounds I was hearing in the woods, and too scared to tell anyone about my anxious feelings. Would anyone believe me? In all aspects of my life, fear was a guiding force behind my actions. I was terrified to live. So why had I attracted a life of fear? The question nagged at me like an infant tugging at the hem of their mother's dress.

I remember the only moments that I ever felt at peace were those amongst the stars. The moments where I would stand in the forest under the dark sky with my gaze fully present on the illuminating sky. I would get lost in the feeling of how grand it all was. The same question many people on the planet wonder as they go about their lives: Why am I here? I wondered more specifically in those moments though, why am I *here?* Here in this very spot, experiencing life through the eyes of struggle, where hard work didn't seem to pay off. How could *this* all be for a reason? Why had I believed so strongly that something special was just around the corner for me? I guess I had been asking, after all, a question that was deeper than my mind could comprehend in those moments.

As the years moved on, my connection to Laure heightened. Her walls represented a part of me that I could not explain. My sorrow reflected within her and the line blurred between who was mourning who for leaving, as we tried to sell the house. I know from my professional training to help people with their emotional trauma that the people closest to us in life often mirror our unresolved unconscious issues back to us. Another form to view what's necessary to heal in this lifetime, a different perspective. The trouble is that most go through life with their eyes wide shut; missing the cues to identify their unresolved pain. I was becoming aware that I had a lot of unresolved emotion around fear and it was evident in each area of my life. My timeline felt intertwined with this home; more than just living within its beauty, and more than just selling her for a profit. Now two years into trying to sell this home, I was becoming more interested in what I was supposed to learn from my time here with Laure.

I had always felt a connection to the forest and wondered if it had healing powers, but I had never really ventured far into its depth. One day, Rob and I took a walk out in the backwoods; he had spent a lot of time there in some of his hardest times and I wanted to share in the renewing energy he seemed to always return with. As we followed the ridgeline up through the towering Maple trees, a calm swept over me. Up ahead was an old stone wall, nearly covered in growth from the forest floor. Stopping for a moment, I relished in the energy of the space; I felt that same connection here as I did to the sky on the nights where my gaze would take me deep into thought. *This is a special place,* I thought to myself. Just then, as I turned to catch up with Rob, I noticed a single large white feather resting on the ground beside me. As if appearing from thin air. A sign that what I was feeling was not a coincidence. A sense of higher connection. This *was* a special place. Grateful for the moment, I hurried my pace to catch up with Rob. My spirit was renewed that day and it was good for my soul.

These years were very challenging, to feel like we did not have control over our own circumstances was extremely frustrating. We had now tried reducing the price substantially, removing all of our belongings, hired a designer and fully staged the home. New marketing was done, and drone video was taken to showcase the grounds. Again, we had a lot of interest and were often asked, "Why is the price so low?" Yet none of the interest came together. We were still in *The Twilight Zone.* What was I missing? It began to feel hopeless and we started to consider abandoning our plans to build on the small parcel of land we had purchased, it had added to our financial strain, but what would we do if we sold it? At this point we were starting to resent the house for not selling, as if it had a mind of its own. We felt cursed to loop in the same cycle of misery. Dumping all of our energy and money into a property that seemed to be the only one not increasing in value; I could feel the heavy onset of the weight it bore on both of us. Rob was struggling to stay above water. Some days he would dip into deep despair and quickly come out of it, other times he would toil for weeks in dark depression. I was beginning to worry about his emotional state again and it consumed my thoughts. Why did I so quickly attach myself to his needs? I had always looked to him for strength, he was my compass to lead the way. So when he was low, my focus immediately intensified on what he needed, oftentimes completely neglecting what I needed. In my dreams I felt a strong pull to him, but still couldn't figure out why the cryptic movements and questioning dialog. We attract into our lives the things we need to heal. My thoughts circled this phrase continually looking for a clue. There had to be a purpose for all of these questions; the key to why we were still here. Looking back, I was receiving my answers, I just couldn't decipher them. My mind was set in the way I had always functioned and I didn't know what I didn't know. Breadcrumbs were everywhere, but I was consuming them as incoherent dribbles, rather than a mass of knowledge spread out amongst each situation. Collectively, I was gaining and storing that mass of knowledge for just the right time.

Chapter Six

PAST LIVES

"gateway in time"

"Sometimes the most evolved souls take the most challenging paths." -Brian Weiss

The terror that night in the moment I woke, from what felt like a memory rather than a dream, stayed with me. Also, the feeling of protecting Rob from something mechanical coming down on him. We were stuck within our current situation of trying to sell a home, which I felt would not let us go, and dreaming of a new future that did not yet exist; I felt in between worlds. My sleepwalking seemed to be getting more frequent and very disruptive. I couldn't rest easy, constantly wondering why this recurring scene was being played out over and over again each night. I needed help.

I had lunch with a dear friend that week and he mentioned one of his favorite books, a curious read called *Many Lives, Many Masters* by Brian Weiss MD, a Psychotherapist who wrote about his experience with a particular patient during hypnotherapy sessions. A patient who had begun to recall traumas from their past lives. Skeptical, yet amazed at this patients' accounting of events from lives described in a different era or culture from long ago, he began to see a pattern. Recurring nightmares had plagued her sleep along with anxiety attacks for many years. As their sessions continued, each time she recalled an experience from a life past lived she made significant progress. Phobias were released and parallels revealed in her healing. It wasn't until Dr. Weiss himself started to receive channeled messages about his own life from "the space between lives" that he would fully grasp the depth of truth in these experiences. It sparked something in me, an intrigue into my recurring sleep movements and life-like dreams. I picked up a copy on my way home that day and couldn't put it down. It was like reading a form of poetry that spoke to my soul. Something said *this is your key.*

I asked around my community of practitioners to find someone who was skilled in performing past life regressions. Now certified with the American Board of Hypnotherapy myself, I had a good understanding of the process that I would undertake and needed someone who was objective. Judith, who has since become like family to me, undertook the task. She lived across the country, but just so happened to be traveling to the area we lived in to run a workshop when I had contacted her. Synchronicity, I was on the right tract.

This is a true accounting of the events that took place during my first past life regression:

"What is your intention for this regression?" Judith asked.

"I would like to understand the source behind my sleepwalking. Specifically the events that are concentrated around my husband Rob, and sister Jennifer," I replied.

The session began. Seated comfortably in the sunken living room of my home surrounded by the warmth of a fire, I closed my eyes. Guided down into a deep trance my breathing suddenly shifted; quick and shallow, I struggled to breathe.

"I'm spinning!" I suddenly called out in a trembling voice, "I can't stop spinning! My chest is very tight. It's hard to breathe."

Judith calmly prompts me to focus on where I am and asks if I can make out what is happening. The spinning stops and I look down to see that I am tightly bound in a string of cloth, my arms and legs wrapped closely to my body so that I could not move. The image was clear and the sensation real, as-if I were there experiencing this moment now in my physical reality.

"What else do you see?" She asked.

"I'm in a cave, it's cold and dark, they've left me here," my voice is shaky.

"Who left you there?" Judith asked.

"The four men who entered the village," my reply was quick, without delay to gather my thoughts. It was as though I had stepped into a movie scene and was on set as a character playing a role. The emotion was real and heightened.

"Who are these men and why are they there?" she asked.

With panic in my voice my breath accelerates, "They came in the night to our village and took me to the cave. I've been wrapped in cloth to keep me here, but I think I can get free," I replied.

"Can you tell what you look like? How old are you? What time period is this?" Judith asked.

"I have long black hair, I am twenty-three years old. It's the 1700s," I described. Immersed in the high intensity of the moment, my thoughts were clear, yet foreign. They felt familiar.

"Can you get free?" Judith asked.

"Yes, I'm trying," I could feel myself struggling although knowing that I was seated without restriction in my current setting, safe in my home. "I'm free," I said. "The cloth was purposely wrapped without tying the end so that I could eventually escape. I was spinning while they had been turning me and wrapping the long strand continuously," I continued with certainty.

"How long have you been there?" she asked.

"All night, it's taken me awhile to get free." I replied. The vision was vivid. As I looked down at my surroundings there was a small fire beside where I had been left.

"Can you leave the cave?" she asked.

"Yes, I'm walking now. The sun is starting to rise. I'm in the forest and there is a pathway," my breath is more calm now and I can feel the cold air on my face.

"Can you follow the pathway?" Judith asked.

"Yes, I'm headed back to my village," I replied. As I could sense getting closer, the smell of smoke consumed the air. "Nooooo!" I suddenly cried out in complete agony. Overcome with an intense heartache and devastation, a feeling I had never felt in my present life before. I cried uncontrollably. "What is happening? What do you see?" she asked.

"It's a big fire, they are all gone. Everything has been burnt to the ground," I sobbed—speaking through my tears. I will never forget that moment. Deep sorrow that was too real to be a dream or made up. As I had neared the end of the path that opened up to a clearing in the woods, the sight of canvas and wood beams that were smouldering on the ground came to view. The memory felt so real as I dropped to my knees. I could feel the dirt of the forest floor within my fingers, as if my home had faded away to reveal another time. A place that once was also my home, where my entire family was burned to death in the night as they slept. They were all gone. Could this be true? Why was it so vivid?

After a few moments Judith asked, "Can you get up? Is there anyone else there?"

"There is no one left. No one survived." I whimpered over my cries. Picking myself up off the ground I gazed over the ridge to see another billow of smoke in the distance. "I need to start moving, leave this place," I said. I recall walking for what seemed like days until coming across another village, "I have found another village."

"Will they take you in?" she asked.

"Yes, they have welcomed me," I replied.

"Why were you taken away to survive that night, do you know?" she asked.

"I am meant to carry a message. I am now in front of people I haven't met before, convincing them of another way," I said, again with clear certainty. "There are children sitting in front of me, listening. I have become one of their leaders. The elders are here and they have accepted me," I continued.

"What are you speaking about?" she asked.

"I can't tell, I can't make out the words I'm saying, but they are important." I replied.

"Is there anything else for you to know here?" Judith asked.

"No, that is all for now." I said with a deep breath.

As I came back to my present surroundings, the energy in the room felt different. The temperature was warmer and I recognized where I was, sitting in my living room, safe by the fire. *I didn't understand what just happened. Did I really just experience that?* We spoke for a while as I explained that I now understood what my dreams had been all of these years; the sleepwalking incidents that focus on my sister and Rob. I was consumed by the feeling of protecting my family as I acted out what I would have done if I had been there to save my family that night instead of being tied up in the cave. I had been hovering over Rob to protect him from the falling, burning structure of our home. An attempt to save my family from burning alive. I knew the instant I came back into full consciousness with a clarity that can only be described as raw, unfiltered truth. The terror and panic, and in those last few nights that I felt "seeing" something mechanical coming down, now made sense. I had been given a glimpse at another lifetime in my dreams; a chance to re-experience what happened and what I would have done if I was given the chance to go back, but I couldn't go back. So, I relived the moment on replay here and now. From that night on, the events stopped. I have yet to experience a night again where I've done these movements over Rob. There were no more feelings of terror or the strong need to protect him. The knowledge resolved the trauma.

During the week of Judith's visit I had decided to take her workshop. It gave me an opportunity to explore more of my inner feelings on connecting with something outside myself. I had started meditating often in different capacities and looked forward to her highly recommended group meditation. As the day went on, I had several moments of clear thoughts for others that were in the group. Moments where I seemed to identify and understand elements of their personalities without tangible information. The thought would appear as any other would, alongside the thousands of other thoughts one has in a day. The difference was, these thoughts stood out to me. Popped up seemingly out of nowhere and when I voiced the information it was accurate for that person, a total stranger. I had relaxed in this setting and allowed myself to be me. The *real me*. The woman who felt connected to enchanted forests and healing powers. I felt safe to be *weird*.

My mom had flown out from Calgary to join me for this workshop. She had always been someone with an open mind and had been struggling with symptoms of chronic concussion syndrome for several years. Although I had never really discussed meditation or energy with her, we seemed to immediately be on the same page. During a break I asked her what she thought on the topic of past lives. Living in the same household growing up, I knew we shared Christian beliefs, and I was curious about her take on the subject. I explained how I thought it could be possible that our souls were here over and over again to learn and grow in each lifetime. Not that we had knowledge of each life here in the present, but that the term *old soul* was an intriguing notion. Why did some people seem to have wisdom beyond their years? To my surprise she was warm and open to the discussion. She believed that if it were possible, that her soul was complete, and she would be going home after this life and nowhere else. Home to Heaven.

We returned into the group and listened to Judith talk about the next exercise. Under a majestic sound bath, performed with singing bowls, we were guided down into meditation. The experience was lovely, calming and I felt like myself again. With my eyes still closed suddenly I saw buffalo running across my inner vision with a sharp taste of blood in my mouth. It quickly shifted to shadows and a dial swept across the screen of my inner sight. Sweeping the image away to the left and circling back. Like a clock turning counterclockwise. I felt nauseous then resumed to normal within moments. Upon sharing my experience a few people looked to each other in the group and said "you're clearing shadow energy." This was my first experience, but not my last.

Shadow energy is not necessarily something evil or demonic, as one might misinterpret, it exists in the emotional turmoil we suffer and can infect the energy of a space unintentionally. It is the heaviness in a room after an argument or in the acts of selfishness above the greater good. There are aspects of each and every one of us that portray shadow energy and learning to integrate these traits from chaos to a higher vibration, such as in love or joy, is crucial to one's personal growth. Shadow energy is attracted to low vibrating thoughts; the ones of self-destruction, pain, anger, and sadness. It feeds on guilt, shame, and fear. Somehow I had a natural ability to detect and transmute these energies in a space. I physically felt the presence in my gut with nausea.

In my curiosity about the spiritual significance or symbolism around the buffalo, I did some research. I learned that it represents the sacredness of life and appears for those in need of strength to endure heavy burdens.[1] Some view the buffalo as a symbol of selflessness or self-sacrifice. In my first experience of seeing the buffalo, I believe that my recent memories of my past life and the pain I felt in losing my family and not being able to prevent their deaths, triggered a form of shadow energy within myself, and my unconscious took control immediately to heal that energy. In my sleep, I had long acted out the intentions of self-sacrifice to try and save my loved ones from their burning homes; sheltering their body with mine. How many other lifetimes had I lived and when did I receive the gift of sensing energy?

---

1   "Buffalo & Bison Symbolism and Meaning," What is My Spirit Animal (website), accessed May 26, 2020, https://whatismyspiritanimal.com/spirit-to-tem-power-animal-meanings/mammals/
buffalo-bison-symbolism-meaning/

Chapter Seven

THE WITCH

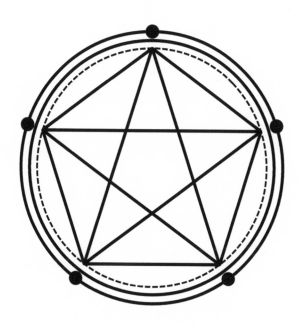

"good vs evil"

What is a Witch? Growing up in a Christian household I thought I had a clear definition of what this word meant. I recall the evenings of October 31 each year at our church where they would talk about Satan and demons and how you must not celebrate Halloween, for you would be celebrating evil and suffering. It scared me and as an adult I held that belief. I've always had a strong faith, but honestly, I didn't feel like I had a good understanding of many things within my religion. As I became more curious in my early thirties, the more questions I asked, the more questions I received. As Carl Jung said, *"It all depends on how we look at things, and not how they are in themselves."* What did that mean? As a professional in the mental health space now, a Neuro Linguistic Programming Master Practitioner, I had developed an inquisitive mind that often took passionate hold of me. I had countlessly said to clients "follow the breadcrumbs," a guidance system I often used myself; after all, those crumbs lead me here to this book you are now reading. So, what did Jung mean?

I wasn't sure why I had such a pull to discover more about what the word *witch* meant, but it kept nagging at me. Like a blister starting to form on the back of my heel. Every time I took a step it became harder to ignore. I believe that the right people, opportunities, and resources will appear in perfect timing; I know this because of the profound amount of times this has happened for me. The key is having a curious mind, you cannot gain the answer to a question you've never asked. As I began to wonder about what it meant to be a witch and why it was presented as someone evil, I noticed my conversations shifting within my circle of friends. I am blessed to have many dear friends, soul sisters, this wasn't always the case though. Not until I was open to receiving that connection in my life did the perfect examples of love and friendships show up for me. I remember meeting Tanya for the first time; I attended a graduates only, support day for professional practitioners in my field. Something that was held every quarter. It was often described as "love fest" because of how much adoration and respect we all had for one another. Avalon Empowerment is the company that I trained with for a substantial part of my skills development and this was one of their events. On arrival that day I was surprised to find that not many of my close colleagues were there. I scanned across the crowd and my gaze landed on a woman sitting in the corner; quiet, poised, and ready to start the day. My immediate thought was *who is that? I should sit with her.* So, without hesitation I followed my instincts, they have proven to be an incredible asset these days. My gut often guided me in the most interesting directions, like an intricate dance blindfolded across a web of glass. I've trusted my intuition to many major decisions in my life and it hasn't failed me yet. So, there I sat beside Tanya, I leaned over and softly introduced myself. We didn't speak much until a break later that day, but I think we both immediately resonated with each other. A few short weeks later, and many rich discussions over coffee, we were soul sisters. Why is Tanya important to my story, to the witch? Our paths are intertwined, as if designed a lifetime ago.

> *"Everything is energy and that's all there is to it. Match the frequency of the reality you want and you cannot help but get that reality. It can be no other way. This is not philosophy. This is physics,"* -Albert Einstein

As with other friends, I had begun to notice the dialog shifting in my conversations, not intentionally, but organically. My energy was shifting and my thoughts were lighter and less clouded. I've had some pretty out there conversations with Tanya; very interesting intellectual and spiritual thoughts have been expressed back and forth between us, but nothing like where this particular chat would go. One day she says "maybe you're a witch." I was immediately taken aback! Everything inside of me said "oh hell no! How could you even say that to me?" These were the thoughts of conditioned Kady. Someone that lived in fear of religion without her own beliefs. Someone who was told to "leave this alone!" as a child, when I expressed that I was speaking with a woman in the basement each night when I wandered my home in my sleep. She immediately sensed the tension in my voice and started to elaborate on the statement. "You do know what I mean by witch, don't you?" Tanya asked me. Before I could answer she started to explain how healers were misconstrued as something negative and were feared for their abilities, so they were cast out, demonized labelled as a witch and killed. *Could this be true? Was there another side to what it meant to be a witch?* How coincidental that I've been so curious about this subject recently, and it comes up now in conversation.

What if my interest and yearning to learn more was to explain some of my own experiences and connection to something beautiful, not evil? Is it possible that many women of the seventeenth century in the Salem Witch Trials were misunderstood healers who were trying to do good, not evil? And why did this matter to me?

As I consumed information about the world's history and the thoughts on the word witch, it appeared that there was a divide on the matter. As with any story, there seems to be two sides to the interpretation of the witch: *"Early Witches were people who practiced witchcraft, using magic spells and calling upon spirits for help or to bring about change. Most Witches were thought to be pagans doing the Devil's work. Many, how-*

ever, were simply natural healers or so-called 'wise women' whose choice of profession was misunderstood."[1]

The modern-day witch in Western society has yet to escape the label bestowed on them in history. Wicca[2] is practiced by most, and in the United States and Canada considered an official religion. Avoid evil at all costs and harm none are two of the main philosophies of Wiccans. This religion is built on fundamentals of peace and balance, while having tolerance for humanity and being one with nature.[3] Why hadn't I heard of this other side before, the healing side.

I've now done a lot of research and asked many questions so here's my personal opinion on the matter; my initial beliefs were shaped by the experiences I've had, but more specifically, by the beliefs of my parents. Being raised in a Christian household was hard for me. I never felt like I could do anything right, nothing was ever good enough and, even when I did what I was told, I was still punished because somehow it wasn't exactly what my father meant. My household was ruled through fear, and most of the time, consequences were relayed as religious beliefs. I learned early on that if you spoke up and voiced an opposing opinion you were punished. The consequence of keeping silence was not developing curiosity or my own values. My individual thoughts and feelings were suppressed. I was conditioned to believe that the things I experienced as a child were to be left alone. Fear of protecting me fueled a shutdown of who I was and the gifts that I naturally possessed—gifts that I believe ran in both my parent's bloodlines.

---

1   A&E Television Networks, LLC, "History of Witches," History.com, updated February 21, 2020, https://www.history.com/topics/folklore/history-of-witches

2   A&E Television Networks, LLC, "Wicca," History.com, updated August 21, 2018, https://www.history.com/topics/religion/wicca

3   A&E Television Networks, LLC, "History of Witches," . . .

In my research I definitely found a lot of reference to how witchcraft was used to summon the devil, cast spells, and create havoc, but there was also another point of view, one with explanations of women who had nothing but pure intentions of helping humanity and healing those in need. The question raised by my experience with Christianity was: are people going against God by practicing healing? Is this act, regardless of intention, blasphemy? I don't believe it is and here's why: mankind was created in the Image of God. I've heard this many times throughout my life. There have been several interpretations of this meaning, but I believe that God resides within our being, and for that to be true, then is it possible that we hold the power to heal ourselves and others? Would it not be by the grace of God or the Divine that someone may be able to heal another? It's a controversial subject and my intention for you is to press the limits of your personal beliefs, not to sway or change your beliefs, but rather to open your thoughts to all that might be possible. There is a part of me that was terrified to express who I felt I was and another part that was screaming to be released. I got to a point where I felt like a complete fraud if I didn't start expressing my true self.

> My truth is this:
> I am a spiritual being;
> I believe there is something far greater than
> you or I holding our existence together;
> I have a purpose to express;
> I am an intuitive leader;
> I am a Claircognizant;
> I sense Energy.

What is your truth? Have you, too, been holding it back from the world? Do you fear judgment from your peers, maybe your family? There have been times where I have been told not to write or speak about my childhood, threatened to stay silent, but that is not my truth and it ate at me until I took the decision back and decided to write my story. I decided to let go of the need to please those around me for fear of being weird and just be me.

My gifts started becoming apparent in sessions with clients. At first, I thought I was just really good at what I did—beginner's luck—that I was able to make connections for each client in their experiences and that it was my ability as a natural listener to help create change for others. Then people started to ask "how did you know that?" during Quantum Change Process™ sessions; these are sessions where I guide a client through a process that allows for clearing of limiting beliefs and patterns that are no longer serving the individual. Again, at first I thought *I'm a trained professional, I'm just good at what I do.* It wasn't until the tenth time that I was asked, and with the look of complete surprise on my client's face, did I start to wonder if there was something more to what I was expressing in these sessions.

I've been blessed to do the work I do. I've witnessed great change in many people after our sessions and I now embrace the energy that I feel working through me. My intention before each session is always the same as I ask, "Dear God, Divine Leader, Archangels, or Universe, please allow for me to deliver the information that this client needs today to move forward in their life, to heal from the hardships of their past and to receive everything that they need to receive today for the highest good of all." I then let go of my own need to "do a good job," for that need is only serving my ego, a part of me that need not be served. Time flies in session and three hours later there is a lightness in the room and I become more of who I'm meant to be each time. There is nothing but love and light in these interactions so how could that be evil?

So, what is a witch? This will still be determined by your perception, personal experiences, conditioning, and interpretation of religious teachings. I believe that there are good and evil forces that surround us but that each and every one of us has the ability to conduct ourselves on the side on which we choose. I believe that a Healer is someone who is divinely inspired by God or the Universe or whatever term resonates most with you, that spirituality and religion are not in opposition, but rather complement each other and amplify the common message; we are all connected; we are all loved; we are all here for a purpose.

"Reclaim the witch, reclaim your power"
-My dearest Tanya Gordon

Chapter Eight

WATER

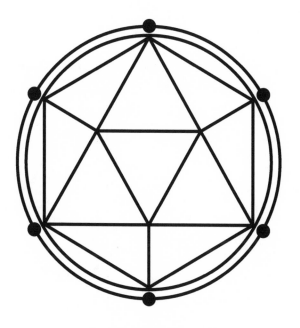

"power of chaos"

Human beings have been known to gravitate toward water; we naturally settle and populate in areas of a water source and ultimately need clean water to live. Throughout history, across many cultures and religions, there's a high significance of water in stories. Christians are baptized in water: Genesis 6:9–9:17 in the Bible, tells the story of Noah and his ark, a vessel that was created to escape the epic flood of earth when the people of the world had become too corrupt. Buddhists will offer seven bowls of water as a gesture against greed, to release selfish attachment.[1]

Water creatures captivate the imagination, from the Loch Ness monster in Scottish Folklore to Kraken, the legendary pirate myth said to swim the deep waters off the coast of Iceland. There's no shortage of tales, so what is our fascination with water and the mystical?

Did you know that water is one of the only attributes of a property that cannot be privately owned? It is typical for a landowner to own up to the shoreline of a body of water or to have riparian rights, but not ownership. Surface water is considered a resource and under common law should be available for everyone's use.[2] It's interesting that many government bodies are highly involved in the distribution and control of water, but is there an underlying reason for this? More than just preserving civilization and social comforts? Somewhere,

---

1   Lee Kane, "Buddhist Water Bowl Offerings as an Antidote to Attachment," Buddha Weekly, accessed May 26, 2020, https://buddhaweekly.com/buddhist-water-bowl-offerings-as-an-antidote-to-attachment/

2   "Lakes and Rivers Improvement Act Administrative Guide," Government of Ontario (website), updated December 10, 2019, https://www.ontario.ca/page/lakes-and-rivers-improvement-act-administrative-guide

deep in our past, did the control disseminate from a knowledge of protecting the natural order within spiritual law?

Water Stories from Around The World is a collection of writings that brings to life the history, and folk stories of water from around the world. It's a fascinating web of tales that gives the reader a glimpse of how water is meant to belong to no one, but rather to be enjoyed by all.[3] As I found myself married to a man that refused to live anywhere that was not on water (no matter the cost) and was drawn to a property that was a rare occurrence of owning the land beneath the water, I began to wonder if the water on this land was more important than just a view, a selling feature to invest in.

Wanting to know more about the history in the area of our new home, the original settlers of the land, and how it came to be that there was a large lake in the middle of a forest, I started inquiring with locals in the area. This tiny community was like an unknown blip on a map, one that only locals knew existed. The original owner had built this exquisite home in the early 1990s with some interesting intentions; from what I've heard through stories neighbors told me, it was an old fishing camp, and the house was a lodge to gather, share stories, enjoy the warmth of a fire, and watch the slow rise of the moon. The owner would sell fishing licenses to local residents and the lake was stocked with Trout. People would come from nearby and often ask us if they could stop for a while and fish, even though we were not running the fishing camp. It made me wonder what happened to the original owner of this home and why his grand ideas didn't survive. I searched further back.

Who owned this land before there was a home on it? I came across an old newspaper article that had briefly men-

3   "Water Fables from Around the World," India Water Portal (website), posted March 12, 2014, https://www.indiawaterportal.org/articles/water-fables-around-world

tioned the area and how settlers had come over from England in the early 1880s. The large lake in the forest was created by these settlers when they constructed a dam across a small waterway to generate energy to operate a local mill, the hub of the community and a focal point for economic growth. The river that once flowed through the valley swelled to cover the surrounding land and the lake was created. Interested in knowing more, I kept searching.

We were still desperately trying to sell the house; keeping up with showings and the maintenance of the grounds was difficult with our busy schedules. We hadn't intended on doing this for years.

I decided to give Judith a call and discuss my curiosity about the history of this land. As we spoke, she immediately felt a strong connection to the water. This land would have held the stories of many families over the Centuries. I wondered how the transition of ownership had occurred each time, and who else might have a history here. I was becoming more and more interested in ancestral lineage and generational healing, not only of my own family but also those who may have been connected to the property. The First Nation community nearby had a long history in the area, well before the settlers of the late eighteen hundreds. I already knew how the waterway was transformed and used for economic growth, so what did it look like before, in its natural state? During our conversation she mentioned the idea of a water ceremony, that perhaps a blessing of the water would put my soul at rest about moving and allow the uneasiness to dissipate. "*You'll know what to do*," were the words that she left me—no direction, just a nod of confidence in my ability to intuitively perform a blessing.

The pieces seemed to fall together effortlessly. I had picked up a copper pot to carry water from the lake to the top of the ridge where the old stone wall sat covered in old forest growth; the place where I felt at peace, where I found the large white feather at my feet. It felt important for me to have someone by my side during this ceremony, so I asked a dear friend of mine to join me. Lucy was another soul sister, I felt we'd spent more than just this lifetime side-by-side. Her face was the first thing I saw in my mind when I thought about how I would carry out this task. The day before, I had gone over to our new parcel of land, where we intended on building and gathered a small chalice of water. It was a beautiful setting. We planned for the home to be built in between two ponds so that we would have a water view from all windows. We had an unshaken bond with the element of water and had been so intent on living near it for all these years. I intended on collecting another chalice of water from the lake that we currently lived on and combining them during the blessing to allow for my heart to accept the transition from one to the other.

It was a cool Fall day as Lucy and I started our hike; it was a quiet walk. Lucy held the two vessels of water separate from each other as I navigated the way. Upon arriving at the spot, we sat connected with the energy of the earth, there was a strong pull of emotion that we both felt. This spot was special and I felt at home here. The air felt lighter as I spoke from my heart to release any pain, regret, or loss. I expressed my love for the land and asked to be able to move forward with ease. The two waters were then combined in the copper pot to be carried to the new property. I had vowed to myself and Laure to do this by my own guidance and not to research how one might do a water ceremony; I wanted to feel with my heart what I needed to do. We drove to the new property and as I poured the blessed water of both properties into the pond, my heart was at ease. I can't explain it, but at this moment I felt connected with the memory I had recalled of my past life. During the ceremony I felt a strong desire to make a donation from the proceeds of our sale to honor the heritage of the land. The earliest information I had of the history was connected to the First Nation community, so I decided to make a donation there when we had completed the sale.

In the days after I did some research on the symbolism of water and performing a ceremony or blessing. To my fascination, there were many parallel aspects to how Indigenous Peoples would perform a water ceremony and what I carried out. How? I had no personal knowledge of this? I went with my gut, my intuition. Had the property guided my instincts by a connection it had to the ancestors? Water has always been considered a sacred element in many spiritual traditions that involve purification or atonement. Had I ventured into a territory within my soul's discovery that needed forgiveness? I had felt as though we were abandoning our dreams by moving and it was as though Laure felt it as well; she reflected it back to me. There was great sadness and anger towards the process of rebuilding the great tribute to what this place once was, only to have her degrade in price and negotiations, and walked away from over and over again. *She* mourned the loss of our adoration for her and couldn't imagine another filling that void. Or was all this just me projecting my sadness and anger onto a structure of mere wood and stone? The feeling was perplexing.

The ability of water retaining memory in some form has been a controversial theory in decades past. Although not scientifically accepted yet, there is an interesting component to the research, the idea that the molecular structure of water could be changed through the process of a blessing. This idea is actually widely accepted in Christianity as blessed water is used to aid in purification and protection; Holy Water.[4] I felt

---

4   Amy Thiessen, "Sacred Water: Connecting to Water Through Ritual and Reverence," Gaia (website), published March 23, 2020, https://www.gaia.com/article/sacred-rituals-connecting-water-through-ritual-reverence

as though the water reflected great sadness and Lucy and I felt the same strong emotion while up on the ridge. Rob and I were approaching year three of the house being for sale and the tiring battle of a seemingly diminishing asset was catching up to us. What was still keeping us here?

As the levels of my professionalism progressed within my practitioner training, this new knowledge was also simultaneously helping me deal with an underlying layer of trauma I still had, related to fear. I was stepping into unchartered territory; an area of my unconscious that had been long buried. I realized I actually had a huge fear of water! How could this be? I had always been drawn to water, I couldn't imagine living anywhere that wasn't surrounded by it, but the truth was, I didn't even know how to swim. I was drawn to the water's edge, but my heart raced wildly with anxiety at the opportunity of being out in it. Looking back, there was a story behind my fear, which seemed to be playing out over and over again in my lifetime; yet it was streaming from my unconscious thoughts from a life, again, lived long ago.

Rob came rushing into the house soaking wet and visibly shaken, I'd never seen him in this state before. He was scared, the look on his face was as if he had just come through battle. He was exhausted and moved past me quickly saying "Go check on Lucius, he fell through the ice!" My heart jumped into my throat and I ran outside into the blistering cold. It was February and one of the coldest winters we'd seen in nearly a decade. For some reason, one of our German Shepherds had decided to walk out onto the middle of the large pond that fed into the lake; it was spring fed and had a constant trickle of water that flowed into the lake just below. He wandered onto an area that didn't typically freeze over. *What had gotten into him?* We had lived there for years and had trained the dogs not to go near the ice. He was okay, wet and cold, but okay. After gaining composure, drying off, and warming up Lucius, I went back to check on Rob.

"What happened?" I asked.

"We were outside near the water's edge and all of a sudden Lucius was out there. He fell through so quickly and I didn't think I was going to get to him in time. I didn't know if the ice was solid enough for me to run out to him. He had fallen straight down through what was only a small opening and was trying to stay treading above water. He couldn't lift his body up out of the small hole," Rob explained, still very shaken up. "I realized I needed something to break the layer of ice between him and I so that I could get out to him," he continued.

"But how?!" I interrupted, as if challenging the idea, like we were there, back at that moment.

"There was a small step ladder nearby that I used to break open a path in the ice from the shoreline. I took the row boat through the path to get to him," he replied.

My thoughts flashed in an instant, thinking how impossible that sounded. Why would the rowboat be within reach? How could he have enough strength or time? This moment will always stand out in my mind. I hadn't truly appreciated what happened that day, how they both survived unharmed without hypothermia. It was a miracle. Rob, oddly enough, had everything he needed in that split moment despite the conditions and the time of year. The row boat had been flipped over resting in the nearby treeline that year instead of making its way to the garage that would have been too far to go and get; a small metal step ladder was with Rob that day, as he had been chopping wood nearby and had used it for a moment to aid him, to grasp with both hands on either side to deliver a strong blow to the ice to break a path wide enough to put the boat in; somehow Lucius had tredded the freezing cold water for twenty minutes waiting for all of this to occur.

Meanwhile, I was unknowingly working upstairs in my office at the front of the house where I couldn't hear a thing. Both of them could have died that day, but that wasn't our story.

We attract into our lives the things we need to heal. I needed to heal my fear of water, but more specifically my fear of ice. I would not have been able to maintain my composure as he had to perform that rescue. The quick moving thoughts that aligned with synchronicity, with the exact tools he had within reach. Lucius has always been a perfect mirror of my emotions; we have a special bond and he picks up on my feelings instantly. His behavior also shifts with those feelings and if I had been out there that day trying to help with my unconscious unresolved trauma around ice, he would have reacted differently. He may not have been able to stay as calm as he did to allow for help to reach him. I now see this moment as an opportunity that I could have had to identify my irrational fear of ice. I hadn't realized the fear or how it had been playing out until something interesting was brought to light in a psychic reading.

The first psychic reading I received was five years after the incident with Lucius on the ice. She was a Medium and a Psychic, which is the ability to connect and deliver messages from loved ones passed and to also see elements of the future. What resonated most with me about this reading was that she read my energetic imprint; she tapped into the aura that surrounded me and was given a clear image. There was no discussion about who I was prior, she just jumped right in. With a big smile on her face her eyes lit up. "This is beautiful," she said, "I'm seeing you skating on a pond. It's a natural setting with trees around. You are dressed in all white and skating in circles, clockwise, almost like a dance. There is a positive significance to your movement in this direction as opposed to circling counterclockwise. You have an amazing energy around you. Three out of three in terms of positive energy."

She didn't know it, but I knew exactly why the clockwise movement was positive. I had already tapped into my ability to sense and clear negative, shadow, or disruptive energy for myself and others around me and that motion was always done counter-clockwise. It made sense that my movements would be clockwise if she felt a positive aura around me.

"The ice represents that you are on a strong foundation, you are very supported in your next efforts," she continued. "I see you in the woods and with water, but the water is more important for you. You are a water person and it's very important for you in your home." I suddenly recalled a memory of a few years back when Rob had taken me out on a surprise day trip. As we were driving he turned and headed towards a local pond that was known for skating, it was a beautiful setting; tall, dark forest pines surrounded the clearing where the water was frozen over. The pond had been cleared for skating and the weather was perfect. He pulled into the parking lot and said, "Let's go, I have our skates in the back." It was a nice gesture and a lovely surprise. As I reached for the handle of the car door I suddenly started to cry. It had been a great day, but my mood quickly shifted to being completely irrational. Refusing to get out of the car, I sat there crying, too scared to move; I was embarrassed, but couldn't help the onset of emotions that were flooding in. Confused, yet respectful of whatever it was that I was going through, Rob left me in the car while he went to skate, figuring I would join him at some point. I never got out of the car that day. I sat crying, filled with fear, unable to get myself to set foot outside of the car. It was the first time that I had ever had the opportunity to skate on a natural body of water.

Why had the memory come to me at that moment? Your unconscious mind will release and bubble up information when it feels safe and ready to do so. There was something about that moment that needed to call my attention towards that memory.

"It's interesting that water is so important for you but yet, I don't see you in water," the woman said. "You don't swim do you?" she asked.

"No," I replied, "I've always been very scared to enter the water. In fact, it even burns my eyes if I get water in them," I told her.

"This is against who you are naturally, do you know that?" she asked me.

I said nothing.

"You are an old soul and your soul is drawn to water. There is an energy here from a past life," she quickly states.

Given my last experience with a past life regression and how healing it was for me I listened more intently.

"I'm seeing that you fell through the ice while skating on a pond in the forest. You drowned. This is a big fear for you and there's more you haven't grasped yet. You are supposed to love water so it's important that you resolve this in this lifetime," she explained.

It was starting to become clear. Why I had the memory just a moment ago about the option to skate on the pond that day but refusing. Why I had felt so much fear. Why the dramatic rescue of Lucius was so important. I was connecting again with a past life. Bringing forth information to heal from a trauma that transcended many lifetimes.

"Learn to swim, skate on a pond, and conquer your fear," she advised me.

Synchronicity yet once again. I had just finished the creation of my signature program in my coaching business— Conquer Your Fear.

Chapter Nine

BRING TO LIGHT YOUR SHADOW

"mystery and knowledge"

There are things that you know about yourself and then there are things that you wish you didn't know. Many people fail to connect the dots on what those hidden things or darker aspects are really trying to tell us. Why do some people experience the same cycles of abusive relationships, self sabotage, and drama? The answer lies within you, I promise you it's there. The fact that you are reading this book is no coincidence. You are drawing in information that is important for your soul's journey. You are slowly awakening and the shadow aspects of your soul are just as important as your natural gifts. Your shadow side offers lessons, not punishment. Bring to light your shadow and regain your power. It's the secrets we hold about ourselves that offer the most value to our greatest potential. You are meant for more than just making it through each day, paying the bills, and trying to survive.

My shadow side presented as a need for recognition; I hadn't realized it but this need ran so deep that it was fundamental to my core values. Your personal values are developed alongside your belief system. One's individual beliefs are developed when the same thought is repeated over and over again in one's lifetime. They are assumptions made based on how we have experienced the world; our early childhood years; ideas we're exposed to repeatedly in a family dynamic; and our parents or caregivers' views (theirs are adopted from their family before them). Think of Santa Claus at Christmas, as a child we are told to go to sleep on Christmas Eve so that Santa may come on his sleigh, flying across the night sky from the North Pole with his magical reindeer to give you presents. His jolly fat body sliding down the chimney with a huge sack of toys to leave under the tree, but only if you were good throughout the year and sleeping when he comes. Did you believe in Santa? Even for just a short time? Chances are, if you did, it was told to you and those around you over and over again until you took it on as truth. Let's think about this even deeper for a minute. Santa flying across the sky in a sleigh powered by reindeer defies all the laws of nature and gravity, and how could he manage to make it to every home around the world in one night? Some families didn't even have a chimney and yet they still were delivered presents. None of that mattered when you were little because the belief held a purpose. It served a part of you that needed the love and attention that the notion of Santa provided. This story also served a purpose for parents; it's said to give children incentive to be good all year round and to go to bed early and sleep through the night on Christmas Eve. Let's not forget the added bonus for parents of cookies and milk left out for Santa that must be eaten to ensure the belief that he was really there. As you've grown up, you've probably adjusted your beliefs around Santa to reflect new information received; knowledge such as the science of aerodynamics and basic time management. That it's physically impossible to have enough time to travel around the world in one night. But, what if you never received this new information? Would you still believe in Santa? As the belief in Santa held true for so many of us, what were some of the personal values derived from this belief? For me it would have been that it's important to be good, for being good meant that you received presents. As all your values begin to form based on the beliefs you hold, stemming from the repeated experiences you've had, where does the shadow side of one's traits start to emerge?

Your emotional needs will always be met, despite what you may think. Let's go back to my need for recognition; this was a fundamental personal value of mine and it played out in my personal and professional life. As I found myself in a job that fed more of who I wasn't and stripped me of any recognition, my unconscious swiftly went to work seeking my core values elsewhere. At the time I had no idea that receiving recognition was even a core value of mine. All I knew was that I didn't feel good in my present role. This was the first sign. Subconsciously searching for a way to satisfy my unmet emotional needs, unbeknown to me there was a part of me that had been sabotaging each and every deal that *should have* come together on the sale of our house. The house had begun to take on a persona of its own; shape shifting into the soul of a woman who craved redemption from her past. I had felt her presence so deeply, but had I created this projection based on my own unconscious self-image? My need for recognition was met through chaos. The drama that came with not selling allowed me to keep *her*, longer. To have a prized possession of note. To live in a spectacular estate that one only dreams of, yet as I had this life and owned these things, my soul was not at rest because the need, and fundamental value of placing importance on recognition, had originated from a darker time in my life. This particular value had been formed around a belief that was not initially my own and it presented as a shadow to face.

My father is a gifted musician and our household was often loud, filled with the sound of him practicing; his drum set was his calling, where his passion lay. I watched my dad put his heart and soul into his music, but never truly realizing his dream. It wasn't a matter of his talent, there was an abundance of that, instead I think the pressure of life and the demands of having a family took over. Perhaps he felt he couldn't pursue the type of life that came alongside being a rockstar? Could it be that raising kids needed a stable income and a father that was home instead of on the road? I watched a talented man never amount to his dreams and I think that rooted deeply inside me. I experienced someone who often showed up angry at the dinner table, could that have actually been resentment for never achieving recognition? I interpreted these experiences as a child as someone who was needing more, someone who was held back from showing up fully as a loving father because he never received appreciation for his gifts. Now as an adult, I had developed a belief around these repeated experiences and it too was important to me, but I had never truly realized it either. This house unconsciously gave me recognition. My needs were being met, just in an unhealthy way that was ultimately causing destruction in my life.

Realizing this set me free. Bringing my shadow to light, the part that served my ego, gave me freedom. I've pulled out the positive attributes that would serve my higher self and the good of those around me, then amplified that core value to serve me instead of self-sabotage. Getting to know my core values in every area of my life has been the catalyst for change. Knowledge leading to self-awareness and the growth in awakening my own gifts has been supported through my own shadow work. Would you like to see where your own shadow could lead you? Could it be your key to unlocking your magic?

Grab a pen and paper if you're curious and willing to bring to light your shadow.

1. **Is there an area of your life that you are currently experiencing chaos or drama?**
   This could sound like, "my spouse doesn't listen to me, they only care about themselves." Could there be a projection of your own actions in that statement? Your unconscious mind will provide hints at the aspects of yourself that need to be loved and transformed. These hints come through as projections onto others, and very often, the people closest to us. Questions you may want to ask your-

self: Is there an area of your life that you are being self-consumed and not open to hearing another's perspective? Is there a time in your life that you felt you didn't have a voice?

2. **Are there traits that you notice in others that really bother you?**

   This could show up as, "why does she need so much attention? It's annoying," when thinking about a coworker. Is there a part of you that was withheld from love and attention? Upon closer reflection is there someone in your life that you wished gave you more attention?

3. **What are your hidden dreams?**

   The ones you don't share outloud for fear of judgement or failure. Do you intentionally play small in life to fit into a role that was pressed upon you by culture, society, or family values? What are the attributes of others who have reached a similar goal or dream? Do you unconsciously have an aversion to those traits? For example; if you want to have a successful business, but have only been exposed to people who lie and cheat their way to the top, you may unconsciously believe that in order to succeed, one must take advantage of others. This could create a block until it's brought to light.

4. **Have you been labelled?**

   Society or self-imposed labels, such as being bossy or too shy, can shed light on your underlying shadow self. Who has taken away your ability to choose? Was there a time in your life where you felt unsafe? Needing control or being unable to speak up can stem from the lack of feeling safe or supported.

As you work through these questions what do you notice? Show yourself the love, patience, and compassion that perhaps was missing in these experiences that shaped your shadow self. The more we know about ourselves the more we grow to understand and accept those around us. The pain of the past is diffused through immersing yourself in the full complexity of a feeling. The emotions in which you may be avoiding, and the trauma associated with it, is where you will find the most healing. The longer something stays hidden or pushed down the more damage it does.

As I released the attachment I had for recognition that presented in my shadow self, I realized that there was one more layer left; I had been working as my own agent in the sale of our home. I was qualified and felt that I would do the best job. What I hadn't initially known was that my need for control over all of the pieces in the sale were bubbling up from the side of me that didn't feel safe. The little girl that was terrified to do something wrong. I needed to let go of this shackle I had created tying me to my pain. I knew what I had to do; I decided to fire myself and hire an agent. I removed my sales representative hat and picked up the seller hat. If gaining a different perspective had continually helped me breakthrough other obstacles in my life, then maybe giving the control to another would allow for me to heal this part too. It had to be someone I trusted, someone who was qualified and objective. I interviewed several agents and made a decision. As she developed a plan and put it into action, I had hope in the future and started to feel free to place my attention on other things. As the property showcased through fresh eyes, we started to gain some momentum, there was an interested buyer who had resurfaced from a previous deal. In all of the former conversations we just couldn't seem to pull things together, but now it looked very promising.

Rob and I had begun to be open to another version of where our lives might be headed. We had been swimming against the current for so long that it was finally starting to sink in. Maybe our story had been rewriting itself over the last three years as I discovered my true path. Working through my levels of fear and resistance to leaving this home had brought me back to myself; I was confident enough to leave the team I was on and create a thriving real estate business on my own; I learned a new skill set in the mental health and wellbeing space and was working with clients in ways that made me feel alive; I started to reconnect with gifts from my past and accepted the parts of me that were a work in process; I attracted a new circle of dear friends that had quickly become family, beautiful souls that supported me in my darkest hours. It was as if an emergency beacon had been launched three years ago, from the depths of my soul. It had been traveling out, rippling throughout time sending out a distress signal that was gathering my salvation. Dropping breadcrumbs in my path to lead me to the next step. Forcing me to wake up, to lean into my pain to understand and forgive myself.

Chapter Ten

THE QUARRY

"a new path"

There seemed to be another tempting morsel of bread-crumbs that were dropping on our path. I had a client that was searching for a lot of acreage with access to a private lake for Bass fishing. After speaking with him about our home I realized they needed more acreage and a deeper water source than our property provided. It was an area of expertise for me and Rob often liked to help with investigating different locations because of his love for these types of properties as well. The options were limited in the direct vicinity and this client was looking for a certain radius to stay within. One day, Rob said to me, "I found the perfect property for your client!" As we went over the details, it was immediately clear to me that this place was not going to work. It didn't have enough acres, the zoning would require a change that would likely not be supported, and it was two hours away from their preferred location. So why had Rob thought it was perfect?

Carl Jung, Swiss Psychiatrist (1875–1961) was known for his work in Perception is Projection; the theory that everything we observe is a projection of something inside of us. Rob was right, this property was perfect, but not for the client he had been looking for. It was perfect for him. This property was exactly what we had been looking for for all of these years! Right down to the tiniest of details. It was as if he had painted a picture of his ideal dream property across a canvas then brought it to life in vivid color. Each and every detail was eerily similar to all characteristics he had been listing off for years. I had given up because I thought it was impossible to find. I explained how it wasn't suitable for the client I was looking for and mentioned how it was a spectacular property, one that we both would have loved. The conversation then dwindled as the thought of relocating and starting over with my business in a new community was too daunting to entertain. Besides, we were still trying to sell our home and had all of our remaining money invested in the land we had purchased a few years prior. It wouldn't have even been financially possible, but Rob's attention toward this property didn't wane, he kept a close eye on it, adoring its every feature.

One of my guiding lights, a response to my emergency beacon had *coincidentally* lived just minutes from this property. A dear friend who had become like family. Over the last year we had talked about how amazing it would be if we lived near one another and how aligned our visions for the future were. How we felt that we had come across each other's paths for a reason. It was really interesting that Rob had come across our dream property right near her. What were the odds? We decided to drive out and have a look at it. What could be the harm? It was a nice drive and I could spend some time with good friends out that way. I figured that once we got there it wouldn't be what we expected in some way and that would be the end of it. There had also been talks of an offer coming in that weekend on our house from the buyer that we had been in discussions with and we needed to try and keep our minds off of it. It was hard not to think of all of the times that all the previous offers had fallen through and how disappointing it was. I didn't want to go down that rabbit hole, it wasn't healthy for either of us. Distraction was a welcomed comfort.

It was a beautiful drive through the countryside towards Kingston. As we arrived at the property, a familiar feeling came over me; my heart raced with excitement as we drove up the long winding driveway to a clearing in the woods that opened up to a massive private lake. The difference here was that there was no home, it was a blank canvas to create exactly what we had been dreaming of. Our current home was far larger than we ever needed. We had hoped to have a bed-and-breakfast there one day where the vast amount of space would have gone to use, but our lives and who we were had now shifted so much that it was no longer what we truly wanted. There was a huge difference with the water as well. The lake that we currently lived on was so large that the boundaries of the water happened to cross into a few of the neighboring parcels of land; meaning that those landowners had access to the surface of the water. Over the last few years, those parcels had been sold to a developer who had built large homes on them overlooking our lake. The once serene privacy of no one in sight was no longer. The water here at this new location was fully contained within the parcels' property lines; meaning no one would ever have access to it; we could maintain the privacy and natural beauty of the shoreline. It was an old stone quarry with beautiful limestone edges that looked like the edge of a mountainside. I had never seen anything so majestic. Then, reality again sunk in, we were not in a position to do this. This was crazy, but we had moved mountains before so maybe something was leading us here. We decided to be open to the idea and that if it were meant for us that we would not force it.

A few things would have to happen with ease for this to feel like it was the right next step for us:

1. We had to sell our other parcel of land.
2. The house had to sell.
3. I would need to have a plan for work that wasn't a compromise to my soul again.

We arrived back home and decided to take action on the things we had control over; These three things would have to align in perfect timing for us to be in a position to make an offer before it was snatched up by someone else. We listed the land we had for sale, to our surprise a cash offer came in with a quick closing. Could this really be a sign? A sign that we were supposed to move forward in a different direction? It was a scary thought to accept the offer. If things didn't go as planned we would lose what we had been working for all these years. It wouldn't be easy to come across another parcel to build on that had a water element. The offer still had not materialized from the interested party in our house and we were very nervous. With my new found barometer of gut instinct, intuition that had led me through many other difficult times, I decided to trust in the process and follow my heart.

As soon as our land was sold we immediately contacted the seller's for the quarry. This next part of the story is where I learned that your dreams can align easily and effortlessly, or sometimes a curveball is thrown to see if you really want it; a test of faith and endurance. Our quarry had been sold to someone else just hours before I called. *What had gone wrong?* My heart was in complete agony. This felt like the right move, that perhaps one of the reasons we had been held back from selling for so long was because we were not meant to build and live on the other property we had bought. Initially, when Rob and I had found the smaller parcel three years ago, it was a compromise to stay in the area. It didn't really meet much of our criteria, but we were trying to make a push to be happier, to live a more modest life and focus on our passion instead of having material things. I had often wondered if buying that parcel of land was the catalyst to our house not selling. Maybe that property was not an energetic match to the work I felt I would continue on to do and therefore living there would not support my highest needs. I felt even stronger towards that theory when the quarry had come into our lives. The investment we made on our other land had grown in value and it allowed us to consider a property that truly was everything we were looking for over the last decade. It was now gone, sold to someone else. The next few days were hard. What had we done? Was this all a mistake?

The emotions that show up while making big shifts in life are very complex. They show up as self-doubt, anger, resentment, guilt, and shame. Often in the form of questioning your decisions and blaming others for why things are not going as planned. I was in the full thralls of this battle; feeling like I did not have control over my own life. What was the purpose of my heartache? The best thing I ever learned was to put a time limit on your self-wallowing. How long are you willing to feel miserable and sorry for yourself? The world will keep spinning and so long as you are in that low vibrating state you will miss your course correction and tailspin. Take the pain and unpack what it's trying to tell you. Open up your version of events to allow for another option to present. "I'm done with this!" I proclaimed. No one is taking away my right to choose my own future. I am responsible for making my own path. My destination was a feeling not a place. Longing for a home that was much more than bricks and mortar, but instead a safe place to be who I truly was.

I picked up the phone and contacted the buyer who had just purchased our quarry; nervous, but determined, I asked them "would you consider selling the property to my husband and I? I realize that you have just bought it yourself, but can I tell you a little bit about us?" To my surprise he agreed! I explained our love for this place and how we had been working towards buying it and somehow we were missed in being notified that his offer had come in. That we sold another property to get there and just missed the opportunity. *Honesty is the best policy. Let go of your ego.* (My heart told me before calling). His response was quick, "you just broke my heart. Yes we will consider it." I was alive again! Blood coursing through every vein in my body. He hadn't known it, but I was outside in our forest that day. In my safe space where the enchanting tall Maples could heal all old hurts. I was supported there and as

I danced amongst the trees that day, with tears in my eyes, my soul was renewed. I was closer to the home of my soul.

Everything seemed to flow after that point. Like a pressure release valve had blown. We bought the quarry and shortly after the perfect family approached us to buy our house. They were gracious, loving, and warm in the negotiations, appreciating every detail of the home. Loving *her* as I had always hoped she would be. Laure was safe in their hands. Accepted, loved, and nurtured. All that she had been yearning for throughout all of these years and I was safe to let her go. We had been intertwined for so long that my emotions ran deep and our connection would always be strong. "You are free to leave," a voice inside me said as a soft whisper, "you have fulfilled your role here and it is now time to step into a new light." What was the new light and why did it feel so important?

We had purchased a beautiful little home just outside of Kingston along the river while our plans for the quarry were developed. I will never forget the day I drove away from our house, Rob had left a month earlier to the new property to get us moved in and set up. I stayed behind because I didn't want to leave her alone until the very last moment of closing day. It was a beautiful time for me. The house was nearly empty of all our possessions and I was able to appreciate her magnificence one last time. The raw beauty of her structure. The house was set far off the road in the middle of the forest where the nights were pitch black and yet I felt safe and secure. My senses were heightened during this time.

Moving day arrived and I packed up my car with my last few items. As I walked the empty rooms of the house I expressed appreciation for the time we shared, I let her know that I understood that I needed to heal from a lot of trauma in order to move forward to my next stage in life and that I understood it was necessary for me to be here as long as we were.

I forgave her and myself for the times I nearly didn't make it through the darkness and wove as much love and gratitude as I could energetically from my spirit to hers into the space. One last blessing to allow her and I to feel safe to embrace a new family. Her family would be the people who would move in and enjoy her renewed spirit, and mine, the beautiful souls that were waiting for me to grow into the person I was meant to be to help guide them on their journey. "Thank you," I said as I drove away for the last time.

Life was shifting. It felt as if this could have all been for a reason, maybe this sharp turn was our course correction. One that dragged on in time to allow for me to connect to the repressed knowledge within me, to allow for my shadow self to surface into the light and use my pain for good. A redirection to make sure that my path was leading to the right destination. Life's hardships were melting away with the promise of a new beginning.

Chapter Eleven

SIGNS

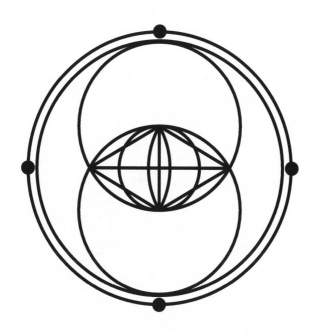

"hidden secrets, unlocked"

The first few days in our new space were surreal. As a child I had moved over a dozen times before I was sixteen, at that time I had finally left on my own for good. I was so joyful some days then deeply sad on others. I had come through a great deal of pain and struggle, but dwelled on it for so long that my muscle memory for pain was deep. *You are no longer in that situation anymore*, I reminded myself and turned my attention to the things I was grateful for here and now, teaching my brain to move forward. Sometimes we get exactly what we need at exactly the right time. The more I trusted that this would be true, the more it happened.

An email came in one day from the buyer of our home shortly after closing; it carried a beautiful message, "you are forever embedded into the fabrics of this place and all the memories we make here." Never, in hundreds of real estate deals that I had encountered, had I seen such a loving energy from a buyer to a seller. Their words were more precious to me then they could have ever known. My mind would wander thinking about the house and wondering how things were going since we had left and this gave my thoughts comfort to rest easy. My home had received a new family with open arms. One that loved her and I hoped she would love them back. I also knew that she would always be with me and I with her.

Shortly after I was attending a Christmas get together. It had been about three weeks since our arrival and this would be a light hearted, fun night where a Medium was to be present and give readings. It was a group of us, all wonderful friends and I was curious to know if anyone would come through for me. I sat silently within the group. The conversation had turned towards me and suddenly became very specific.

"This is a bit odd," the woman said with a puzzled look on her face.

"I'm sensing a woman, almost like she's roaming the rooms of your home," she continued.

Immediately my heart started to race. Was she talking about a spiritual connection I had in my sleep when I had once used to roam the rooms of my house? I said nothing, but was holding back emotion.

"She's not a loved one passed," she says, "does this make any sense to you? It's a bit odd to me."

I felt I did know what she was talking about, even though it didn't make 100 percent sense, so I nodded my head yes. What no one knew is that I had recently been battling an overwhelming feeling of conflict within me, I hadn't shared this with anyone yet, but I had been having more and more experiences in one-on-one sessions with clients where I seemed to have information or *clear knowledge* that I *should no*t have. Moments where I allowed my ability as a Claircognizant to flow through. These moments were insightful and specific to the progression of someone's journey that was in session with me. When I allowed myself to speak the knowledge that had suddenly come to me it always had a meaning for the person I was working with. My intuition was heightening, but at the same time, I was conflicted within my childhood religious views. I was in a state of fear. Scared that if I was having a connection to something and if I allowed it, that I would be allowing in something dark as well. All of my experiences had been positive and meaningful so I felt completely out of alignment to ignore my instincts. I had recently been wondering if the times in my sleep where I would walk about in the house were connected to me embracing this gift. In my sleep I was not consciously resisting my thoughts and many times my dreams had meaning to what was going on around me. In those times it was as if my body needed to act out the information that I was receiving because my conscious mind was holding me back from speaking. The energy had to be released.

"I feel like this is your spirit guide and she is trying to help you to connect with your gifts," she suddenly said.

The conflict I was feeling was starting to make sense to me. I had a strong intuitive pull to express the information that I occasionally received, but held myself back out of fear of judgement. Judgement of those around me, my family and society, but also from God. My views on God, however, had also recently opened up. I had experienced a lot of pain with religion and rejected much of my higher spiritual connection because of the complex association I held with that pain.

"There is a deep sadness within you so know that she is still with you," the woman says, "guiding you to open up."

Words I had needed to hear, and ones that only made sense to me. I had often described sleepwalking like I was living through someone else's eyes. Like I was trying to un-cover something or hear something that was being said to me. I felt as if I was always in a state of curiosity in my sleep. Could it be that in these times I was connecting to my spirit guide? Trying to learn what I needed to know about myself. I had felt such a beautiful, strong, feminine energy with me at times. All of these years as I had faced many challenges, different homes with odd and interesting situations, each one had led me one step closer to this moment of clarity. It had always been in times of heightened stress, fear and worry in my life that my sleepwalking was most active. Could it be that my spirit guide was with me most in those times? I had experienced that feeling for so long in our last home that I was now longing for that connection since the stress had subsided. It suddenly dawned on me that if this were true I hadn't been allowing her connection unless I was experiencing emotional trauma. I left that day with the decision that I would be open to receiving. That I was supposed to experience the things I did to connect to something greater than I and that I was meant to use these gifts rather than hide from them.

The Universe, God, or whatever word that resonates best with you, has a funny way of showing you exactly what you need to know. Messages, nods in the right direction, and synchronicity when you're on the right track. Synchronicity is a concept first introduced by Carl Jung. A "meaningful coincidence" where random events seem to line up in ways that are too intriguing to ignore.[1] I experience synchronicity in moments where I'm on a trail of breadcrumbs; moments where my thoughts align with my soul's desires, whether I'm consciously aware of that desire yet or not; moments where I'm focused on thoughts that feel good and not clouded in doubt or fear.

It was two months before closing day and an opportunity had presented itself to visit a labyrinth located north of the city. A labyrinth is a circular designed pathway that's intricately designed for a person to walk to the center of the design and then back out again. This is done in a calm setting and is much like a meditative process that allows for one to clear their mind and reflect on a specific intention. In spiritual practices it represents the journey back to being whole; to go within for the answers. I was heading into a major turning point at the time leading up to the move and I was looking for clarity on my higher self-connection.

That day, as I held the intention of clarity around my spiritual connection, I entered the labyrinth. It was a beautiful walk with deep colors of the Fall leaves surrounding the edges in the circle, stones lined the pathway to a small opening where you could rest to contemplate the thoughts and mes-

---

1   "Synchronicity," Wikipedia, last edited May 21, 2020, https://en.wikipedia. org/wiki/Synchronicity

sages received on your journey in. As I circled the path into the center, pausing to reflect, I had received a repeating message—*Red is important.* It didn't make any sense to me, but I kept thinking the words over and over again. As I walked the path out again at every turn my thoughts ran deep on the color. It wasn't a color that I particularly liked, actually, I hadn't even owned a single thing that was red. Why would it be important to me?

I shared my thoughts later with a friend and the phrase that had circled in my mind—*Red is important.* A breadcrumb? Some research revealed that the spiritual significance of red can relate to feeling safe and having security in your surroundings. During periods of change in one's environment, seeing red can be symbolic that more is happening beneath the surface than meets the eye; that one is supported in their next steps.[2] Red has been said to be the only color that spirits can see, and reflects blood, power and energy. In wearing the color red one hopes to call back loved ones who have passed. A red dress hanging in solidarity is a symbol to call awareness to the staggering number of missing and murdered Indigenous women and girls. In Hinduism red is a sacred color that is often used in ceremonies, and for protection.[3] A chill sent through my spine. I had gone in with the intention of clarifying my spiritual connection. Is this why I felt a strong desire to donate money from the sale of our home to honor the land? Was the land holding a story that was still felt through sadness and struggle? Had something happened there?

Shortly after the move was complete, I traveled back to the area to give my donation. The hours leading up to that moment held an interesting energy. The night before I had

2 Crystal Clear Intuition accessed July 5, 2020, https://crystalclearintuition.com/spiritual-meaning-of-red/
3 accessed July 5, 2020, https://wou.edu/wp/exhibits/files/2015/07/hinduism.pdf

taken a picture of the check that I would deliver. More of a keepsake than anything, but as I snapped the photo the image suddenly flipped on the screen. Confused, I took another thinking there was something wrong with the lense. No change, this time the image stayed as I had taken it. In angel or oracle card readings, sometimes you'll pull a message card in reverse or upside down, this immediately reminded me of that. There are several ways to interpret a message that is pulled in reverse. My interpretation has been that there is importance in the message of that particular card pulled. It could be highlighting an area that needs special attention or it's significant to one's personal journey and discovery of true self. I had already felt like donating this money was important so was this confirmation? A sign?

Arriving that day, I stayed in the car for a few moments to slow my breath and center my thoughts. I didn't know what the money should be used for, but it was one of the questions that had come up from the Chief before my arrival. My only thought was to say wherever it was needed most. I walked into the building and after a short reception handed the check to the Chief. With a smile she said, "the Elders are all around us and they are smiling. There is good energy on this money." It was a lovely moment and I was grateful for the beautiful feeling it brought to me. Afterwards I asked the Chief where the money would be directed to.

"The archeology department," she responded.

"What specifically does the archeology department do," I asked.

She proceeded to tell me how the money would go towards the proper care and blessing of remains discovered on private properties when disturbed by new development. I immediately thought of the color red and the significance of finding and allowing for the remains of loved ones who may have been missing to be put to rest. I instantly knew that the money was going to the right place. It was a quiet drive home that evening with a bright round moon ahead of me in the sky.

I had been carrying my notebook that day and had dropped it into my purse on the way out the door in the morning; it was more a journal where I jotted down ideas and stories when they flowed to mind. I had taken it out of my purse and placed the book on the seat of my car earlier in the day. Upon arriving home I picked up the mail, grabbed my book off the seat, and headed into the house. In my office I slid the notebook back onto the shelf where I had taken it from, but noticed that there was something tucked in between the pages making it too tight to fit in the spot. As I peeked inside the pages, two small round stones rolled out; black obsidian stones. *Where had these come from?!* I was surprised. Black obsidian is a natural stone that's formed from volcanic lava. It's known for being a protection stone, one that allows for truth and an aid in grounding one's self. It has a very metaphysical presence and air of mystery with it's glass-like surface. Some believe it has healing properties and the ability to shield from negative energy.[4] I had been writing about my thoughts and feelings towards my gifts being revealed on these pages and it could not be a coincidence that these pages now had protection stones tucked within it's center.

It was not the first time I had received a protection message guiding me to pay attention, that I was supported, and on the right path. Since the beginning of my journey to here and now writing this book, I have received a spectacular display of angel and guiding energy. We were in the second year of trying to sell the house, the tension was so thick within the walls of the house that it was suffocating to be within.

4   Rodika Tchi, "How to Use Black Obsidian for Healing and Good Feng Shui," The Spruce, updated October 27, 2019, https://www.thespruce.com/black-obsidian-use-in-healing-and-feng-shui-1274369

One day, upon arriving home there was something on the outside of the window. The main floor had massive floor to ceiling windows and there was a huge imprint of a fully out-lined wing span. The details were impeccable. Stretched out over two feet each feather perfectly defined. Wings have been known to symbolize freedom and spirituality, a message from God. A tattoo of wings is common to show remembrance of a loved one passed. I sign of divine guidance. It was a capti-vating sight that stayed for weeks perfectly preserved on the glass until finally washing away in the rain. Had a large bird perfectly planted it's image in dust on our window or was it a sign? I'll never really know, but the odd occurrences through-out my life were adding up.

Thinking back to the reading I had experienced where my energetic imprint was viewed, there were so many more con-nections. Expressing that I was a healer many times over in other lifetimes and that I was being directed to help remem-ber my skill. She had talked about my calling being within a modality that was hands on; she had no idea at the time that I was working in Quantum Change Process™ sessions with a hands on approach through muscle testing. I had studied the theory of generational trauma and had worked with cli-ents through the struggles they had faced with cycles of abuse through the family. In my experience, there was a correlation of emotional damage to trauma experienced in generations past; unresolved negative emotions around traumatic events influencing the behaviors of family members. Not only those directly affected, but also family members that carried forward the beliefs from stories or feelings around another's behavior. I had dealt with many cases of this through my work as a prac-titioner and wondered if the same could be true for positive experiences and spiritual gifts. Could my parents have carried forth generational knowledge of a spiritual connection from our ancestors?

I took a trip out to spend some time with my mom and to dive deeper into her past; I had a feeling that there was more to her personal beliefs that could shed light on who I felt I was growing into. She had been so open to the experiences and conversation we shared at Judith's workshop and I suspected that she had an interest that stemmed from before I had introduced it. As we sat and talked she leaned over and said, "you know it's really interesting the work that you're doing. I've always been so interested in everything you're learning, and I feel like you're living my dream."

She told me stories of meditating in her younger years and of family members who she had felt carried forward intuitive gifts through the generations. We talked about her experiences in her dreams that carried messages and reoccurring scenes much like mine. She even told me how she had heard the orchestra music at points in her life as well. I had been practicing intuitive writing, where after a still meditation I allowed for my thoughts to flow fluently and to just write without filter or conscious direction. A practice that she shared with me that she had also done for years. It was like I was picking up where she left off without her preparing me. It was happening organically. It was as if the first half of my life I held myself in resistance to becoming my true self. I had held onto pain, struggle, and trauma for as long as I could until my ancestral lineage found a way to break through.

This conversation unintentionally took place on Palindrome Day; a day where the date reads the same both forwards and backwards. 02-02-2020. The last time this occurred was 909 years ago on 11-11-1111 and would not happen again in our lifetime. A spiritually significant date in terms of energy. Two is known for being highly connected to divine feminine energy. In the Bible, Eve is number two. There is a harmonious energy to two and it can represent a major shift and new beginnings. It was an important day to reflect and meditate on the intentions of one's goals and future dreams. A perfect day for this particular discussion. Synchronicity at it's finest. Numerology and the sequence of numbers and how they relate to one's purpose in life was an intriguing concept to me. I was continually seeing repeating numbers and was interested in how it was all connected. As I transitioned into my new surroundings the number two was everywhere. I'd glance down while driving to see 222 kilometers travelled on my odometer, my heating bill was $222.22 and my ticket pulled as next in line to renew my driver's licence read #222. Through what some call angel numbers or numerology I was being reassured that balance was being restored to my life and to keep following this path. Shortly after embracing the notion of being receptive to connecting with my gifts I started seeing three and the repeated sequence everywhere. It made perfect sense. Three represents the presence of spiritual masters or leaders to guide and encourage. As a Biblical interpretation 333 has been said to indicate that Jesus is with you and to have faith. I was aligning with a higher sense of purpose and that was being reflected back to me through numbers and signs.

Chapter Twelve

SOULMATES AND CONTRACTS

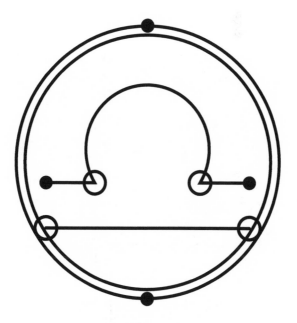

"our shared sign"

There is an unseen energy that attracts people together through vibration, alignment, and destiny. Two souls that are destined to meet will find themselves on an intertwined path regardless of distance, time, or circumstance. It had always felt as though Rob and I were on a predestined course to meet; we had lived through the most challenging of times and our connection was stronger than ever. I had supported him during his darkest hours; depression that ran so deep that he had nearly succumbed to it. He had experienced the breakdown of my old self and allowed me to grow into who I am today. Without each other we would be on very different paths, but that was not our story. Our story is one of love and respect that mingled across the stars long before our present time. We shared strange quirks and appreciated the same inside jokes.

I have a large birthmark on my side that appears as a darker semi-round area of skin. One day it suddenly started bothering me. It was like a nagging pain that was concentrated just on that spot, almost like a bruise. It had never bothered me before and I rarely even remember it being there. Rob, too, has a similar mark on his side and I had always joked between him and I that it was the mark that connected us from another lifetime. These comments were made well before I had any knowledge or experiences of past lives. It was just a strange thing we both had. Reminded of its presence because of the pain, I asked him, "do you ever have any pain around your birthmark?" His response surprised me, "no, except for the last few days." We were oddly both experiencing a similar feeling at the same time. Coincidence?

A few years later in my energy reading with the psychic medium she had brought up my husband; I hadn't said I was married, nor brought him up myself. I already knew our connection was special and he wasn't really a point of interest in my mind that day, but, nonetheless his presence came through.

"Your hubby is a cool guy! He's a very old soul," she said out of nowhere. "You have shared many lifetimes together, yet this is your first romantic relationship," she continued, "you feel very safe around him because he's been your protector and mentor many times over."

I was hearing what I already felt to be true. My life that I had experienced prior to him had been filtered through fear and low self-worth, but my energy was transformed in the presence of his. My soul was safe with him, I knew that to my core from the moment I met him. We talked about how he was beginning a year of completion and tying up loose ends while I was entering a new phase that was all about connecting with spirit. At this point I was well aware that I was on a path to connect deeper with myself and a higher wisdom and this was just another sign. As a timeline converges with another, do you believe it could be destiny? Is it possible that we enter into a soul contract with one another to fulfill? I believe that the people we attract into our lives have great purpose and lessons to offer. Has someone ever made a significant impact on your life? What did they offer you that you needed?

Here are the key points to identifying if someone in your life may have a soul contract with you:

1. Their actions have had a significant impact on your life for the positive or negative.
2. Your lives seem to be connected through a meeting by chance or synchronicity.
3. They appear in your life during times of personal growth.

4. They challenge your thinking patterns or create curiosity within you.
5. You may be drawn to them purely by their energy or charisma.

Some of my greatest life lessons have been from people who've had a negative impact on my life. Negative in the sense that if their actions were taken out of context and without compassion, they would be considered abusive and controlling. Upon closer examination, they were very hurt people trying to reclaim their own power that had been taken by others in their life, in whichever way they had been taught. We live in a world where vicious cycles of hurt people hurting others has become the normal release of negative emotions and past trauma. Little boys have been taught not to cry to avoid the label of being weak, while little girls are told to smile and be polite even when their gut instinct is to say no. The cycle is perpetuated forward for so long that by the time someone tries to understand their actions they are often disconnected from the original trigger that set off the drama.

When you can take a perspective from outside of yourself to discern; *what does this have to do with me?* One's negative experiences will hold a lesson. That does not mean that what the other person did was okay, nor does it mean that you did something wrong. *What does this have to do with me?* Is a checkpoint, a chance to realize a lie that is running and stop it in its tracks before the cycle of hurt is carried forward to the next person on your path.

I have been made stronger through my experiences and without them I would not be the person I am today. Someone who is living their life *on purpose* with so much gratitude. The grit in between my coats of paint were left for a reason. The time I spent on the layers in between my color allowed for the hues of life to radiate brilliantly, rather than dull and rough.

I gained self-love and appreciation of my own quirks in these times, and allowed my strange qualities to blossom without self-judgement. Without the journey in between I wouldn't have the compassion and patience necessary to hold a safe space for my clients in their breakthrough work. What you may think makes you weird is likely the very thing that makes you special; a unique quality that is key to your life's purpose.

If you haven't yet realized your unique traits that make you special, look at the things that you think make you weird and examine your beliefs around those traits with a different perspective. There are questions provided for you to work through following this chapter; do these with compassion for yourself, understand that your views are adopted from your experiences, and most importantly, how you feel about your experiences. Two people may have the same experience, but their internal dialog around the situation may vary, therefore eliciting different emotions. Your internal dialog and the image that you ultimately create in your mind to categorize an event and make sense of the information is a very unique process; no one else does this the exact same way as you. With the massive amount of information that we are bombarded with each moment, it would be impossible to take in and internalize it all. This information comes through all of our senses in the way of what we see, hear, smell, taste, and touch. Our brain will then filter that information through our internal programs. These programs are like your computer's software; they are made up of your personal beliefs, values, memories, decisions, and data you've collected up until that moment. In order to process all of that information as quickly as the mind does, and to formulate a response, it must generalise, delete, and often distort the information to break it down to a more manageable amount of data. From there, an internal representation is given; this representation is unique and can vary widely from person to person. That internal image, thought, or feeling will in turn provide a state; or disposition. That state of mind translates through your physiology and ultimately produces a behavior. All of this happens within moments. Fascinating, right?

Can you remember a time when you had a conversation with someone and you found out afterwards that the person told another about what you talked about, but their accounting was completely different than what you had said? We've all experienced this and it can be frustrating because you know what you said, and that's not what is being repeated. The natural communication process and our internal programs are the cause. The other person may have very different internal filters that the conversation is passing through, which is directly influencing their result of the information, or in this case, the way they tell the story. It doesn't mean that they are necessarily telling an intentional lie, it could just be that their internal representation of what you said produced a different result than yours. It can be tricky waters to navigate in a disagreement.

Identify your unique traits—the key to living your life's purpose:

1. What trait do you consider to be different or weird that you have? Keep in mind that you don't have to relate them to being good or bad, just something you identify as different.

2. What do you think OTHER people think about these traits? What do you tell yourself that others are thinking?

3. Who are the people that have these beliefs about this type of trait? Where would you encounter them? Do you know anything about how they have

adopted this life view? Was religion, society, culture, age, or sexual orientation a factor?

4. Do you share these same beliefs or could they be assumptions or *mindreads* of what you think you are being perceived as?

What did you learn? What questions do you have? What else do you need to know? The point of these questions is for you to start examining your own thoughts and feelings around your perception of the judgement from others. Is it possible that what you think is weird is actually a projection of unresolved emotions around a particular belief that is not serving your highest purpose? Could your traits be an aspect of your shadow self that could offer great insight on your path to wholeness?

As I stepped forward into new shoes in a new setting feeling supported and guided on my path, I still encountered a few stones along the way; the difference became that instead of tripping, falling on my face, and crawling through the dirt, I simply observed the stone and stepped over it. The strangest lesson we are all here to learn is that there is no final destination on this earth. Regardless of your beliefs on where we go after, or if our soul returns in another life, there is one thing that will remain the same—change is unavoidable. You will make plans, have goals, and then decide that you'd like to do something else. Follow those breadcrumbs, allow yourself to change. Don't wait for the jackhammer to pound the ground around you to force your foundation out from beneath you. Look for the signs and observe the soul contracts. Make a choice and accept that life is a journey. Look for synchronicity and numbers. Believe that *"miracles come in moments. Be ready and willing"* (Wayne Dyer). As I reexamined the last few years through the lens of curiosity for signs, soul contracts, spiritual connection, and synchronicity, something stood out.

A feeling that was deep within me; a *knowing* that felt true yet puzzling—I had unfinished business. Something was calling my attention, speaking to a part of me that had no ears to hear, no eyes to see, but only a place to know; my soul. Something was calling to my soul and it was making a desperate plea for help.

Shortly after selling Laure, our lake house, I felt like there was something missing. We had worked so hard to move past our financial hardships, disappointment, and health crisis that it was an odd feeling to have moments of complete sadness. I was confused and felt very drawn to engage back with my memories of my time spent in our previous home. There was one resounding question. Had I picked up all of the breadcrumbs? Was there something left to know and understand for why I was so drawn to that house and why it took us so long to leave? There were pieces of information that I was receiving in flashbacks. My dreams were vivid with information and thoughts that seemingly had no meaning before, but were pushing their way to the forefront. It felt like someone was communicating with me. Did I have another soul contract that I hadn't been aware of yet?

The presence was female and came through strong. The feelings she presented me were deep sadness and loneliness. She was quiet yet persistent. It were as though her thoughts were in my head, but I had no understanding of who this was or why I needed to know that she felt isolated and needed help. My visions held a woman with blue eyes and pale skin much like my own. Was this just the reminisce of an unconscious feeling of my own. Some clean up work from the last few years? I wasn't sure, but it felt like more than that. I had been learning to trust my gut, follow my instinct, and believe in the power of spirit. Now was not the time to dismiss these feelings. I sat down to clear my mind and write out the thoughts that had been coming to me. These were the repeating phrases:

> There is a woman who feels she needs the truth
> to be exposed.
> She led a controlling life in fear.
> She wants you to know that she is still with you.
> She is still there and hasn't been forgotten.
> You are closer than you think.

A chill ran straight through me. From the center of my chest through my body to the floor. I suddenly remembered a few years back when we had met a local trapper in the area where we had lived. There had been a licensed trapper for years who came around once a year and asked for permission during hunting season to access our property. We had allowed it, but then one year he disappeared. We hadn't heard from him and thought it was a bit odd so Rob made a friendly call to check in. The line was disconnected. Thinking that was a bit strange we asked around and heard that he had suddenly left the country. The next year I was visiting a good friend 3400 kilometers away and the topic oddly came up. It turned out that another friend of hers, sitting beside me whom I had just met that night, had a brother who was a trapper and he lived minutes away from me. Coincidence? I thought not. The brother had been looking for somewhere to train their hunting dog and our place was perfect. We probably wouldn't have said yes to allow access if the other trapper was still active, but since he was gone we agreed. A few weeks later I was back at home and Rob and I met the new trapper for the first time. He had an interesting story to tell us. It turns out that there used to be a small cabin at the front of our property years ago. It was the original home that the person who built the lake house resided in during construction. The trapper told us that he now owned that small cabin. It was taken off the land and relocated to his place. Another coincidence? What were the chances of meeting someone through a friend of a friend on the other side of the country that owned a piece of history to our property? The bigger question that circled my mind was why was this memory so vivid to me now. Why was it being highlighted with the thought of a woman who needed to expose the truth? What was I being called to find out?

Had the home we had just moved from held a secret that was just being revealed to me? Was someone guiding me to find them? When we enter into this lifetime I believe that we have a purpose. A decision is made to fulfill a need for our soul to grow through lessons and experiences. In order to fulfill that purpose we agree to certain things with other souls. Other beings that have their own purpose that is intertwined with our own. These soul contracts are inevitable; predestined. With all I knew at this point in my journey this felt like one of those agreements. As I sorted through the flashes of information and collected coincidences, my breath became heavy and I felt a sudden downpour of information. I didn't know how, why, or when this occurred, but I suddenly realized that I thought a woman's soul was captured within the walls of that home. That the structure had become the home of her soul and I was meant to find out why she wasn't able to move on. It was like the woman in the basement all those years ago at 1338, my childhood home. Someone was trying to connect with me and this time I wasn't going to run away. Maybe all of the odd experiences I'd had throughout my life were attempts at others trying to communicate with me from beyond our physical reality. Had I been pushing aside and rationalizing these moments out of fear? Perhaps now was the time to embrace this gift to communicate and discern this information rather than be frightened by it. In various homes, hotel rooms, and friends and family's places, I had experienced kitchen cupboards and closet doors opening on their own, large pieces of furniture moved in the night, area rugs turned upside down, and walls seemingly crying; streaming with water when there was no rain outside. I had heard countless unexplained sounds and one thing seemed to always stay consistent. They were concentrated around me, these experiences followed me and not the structure they occured in. Again I questioned, has it followed me my entire life? The answer was a resounding yes, and someone needed me to embrace this gift in order to help them.

Chapter Thirteen

SARAH

"divine feminine power"

As I continued to evolve my new life in a new city, opportunities opened up for me to share and help others on their journey, but I still had moments of doubt. Showing up to speak in front of hundreds of people to share intimate details about my strange encounters, while dealing with feelings of low self-worth and self-sabotaging habits, was hard to embrace. So how did I push past that fear and continue to show up when each opportunity presented itself? I had to kill my former self; the girl who believed that she couldn't do anything right had to die so a new version could emerge to fulfill her life's purpose. Her messy web of negative emotions that fed her destructive self-talk would not support the life I wanted. Through the ashes of what was torn down, an alter ego appeared that encompassed my true self; one that had emerged from coincidences so intriguing that confirmation was everywhere. The more I aligned with who I was naturally, without the judgement of others and confines of religion, or the trauma of my past, the more I experienced synchronicity.

In the days leading up to the morning that I arrived to donate money from the sale of our lake home, I'd had several discussions with the administration about the details of my arrival that morning; where to go and to whom to make the funds payable. The name "Sarah" first showed up for me on the heels of my donation to the archeology department. When I walked into the building I said to the woman who greeted me that I was Kady and was here to give the donation.

"Oh yes, they are expecting you. I'll let them know you're here," she politely said. She picked up the phone and said, "Sarah is here about the donation."

When she hung up the phone, I gave her a slight smile and said, "no it's Kady, remember?"

Her eyes widened, realizing she had said the wrong name. "I'm so sorry! I have no idea why I said Sarah," she replied.

It was no big deal, but something stuck with me at that moment, a small tingle had run up my spine when she said it. It felt familiar and I was curious about why the name rolled off her tongue so matter of factly, and further, that the person on the other end of the line knew that she meant me.

The days after I was bombarded by the name everywhere I went, as though to say *pay attention to me, remember Sarah.* Every appointment I had from new clients, to meetings and acquaintances I met that following week were named Sarah. I was looking for a new hairstylist one day when a friend sent me a message that read, "Sarah is definitely your girl."

Okay I'm listening! Who is Sarah and why is she important?

Practicing meditation has made a beautiful impact on my life. Oftentimes it's a highly metaphysical experience for me. I've learned how to navigate my feelings and Clairgognizant information that I receive. I quieted my mind and asked the question from within—Who is Sarah and why is she important? Immediately I was surrounded by a divine feminine energy; She had a name and it was Sarah. She was the part of me that had stepped into her power and radiated an energy that could move mountains. Sarah was strong and confident and ready to be embraced. She embodied the feelings I had in the times where I felt really empowered. Allowing her energy to flow through mine, to wash away doubt and self-judgement, gave me an instant switch to flip. When I envisioned Sarah within me, I elicited my true self; a woman who was empowered, self-assured, and loving towards herself and all others around her. She lived in the place where my soul was created, and residing in her energy felt like home. Connecting with her allowed for my gifts to heighten. Now was the time for Sarah to emerge. She was my alter ego; the side that existed when I dropped the mask; the persona that stepped forward with power, grace, and magnitude. She represented all of what I knew I could be if I didn't limit myself. Instead of wondering what my life would have been or who I could have been if things had gone differently, I could be that person now, at any moment by eliciting Sarah. I could live my truth anytime and embrace the home of my soul. She was my higher self.

I was still curious about why this specific name seemed to feel right. I hadn't really known many Sarah's in my life who might have had an impact on me. As my state of curiosity sat with me, my internal guidance system had sent off a beacon to find the answer. Soon after I was drawing in information from resources that I hadn't been physically searching for; synchronistic conversations where someone would randomly mention a story about a Sarah, or ask "hey, did you know . . ." then share an interesting tidbit of information about something relevant to an iconic Sarah. There have been some pretty significant women named Sarah throughout history and compelling energy behind each story.

In Genesis 17:16 of the Christian Old Testament God said to Abraham that his wife Sarah would be "a mother of nations." There are many references to her in different faiths where she is depicted as a spiritual woman or prophetess. On the opposite spectrum, Sarah Good was one of three infamous women who were prosecuted for witchcraft during the Salem Witch trials in the 1600s. She had claimed her innocence right until the moment of her death; some believe that had she confessed, she may have been spared her life. Her conviction and ability to not be swayed in her terrifying last moments stood out to me. Having lived much of her life in poverty, she struggled greatly in her time; while imprisoned, she gave birth to a daughter who she named Mercy, a small glimmer of perhaps what she was asking for from the powers that be. The name Sarah also means "woman of high rank."

Sarah Bernhardt, or often referred to as the Divine Sarah, was a famous actress in the late 1800s through the early 1900s. She was a very talented woman who went on to open her own theatre company, but she wasn't an immediate success.[1] She was a strong woman who made her mark by consistently staying true to who she was without compromise, despite facing many challenges, she didn't let anything get in her way on the path to realizing her dreams.

The powerful attributes of these three women combined are who I embody as Sarah. Guided with pure intentions and a connection to more than myself, I draw from Sarah, wife of Abraham; with steady endurance, confidence, and a clear message, I draw on Sarah Bernhardt; standing strong, refusing to waiver to persecution, I draw on Sarah Good, who may have been a healer of her time and falsely accused. My perseverance had led me to her and the lake house was the heart that cracked everything open.

So my secret to showing up with confidence and in my power is Sarah; I guess she's no more of a secret now than the color of the sky. I found myself in her and it took for me breaking into a million pieces, to be confused, uncomfortable, and to some days feel like I was walking through fire to reach her, but I found her. We are very complex, yet simple beings. We make things hard and only see challenges when we don't necessarily have to. We ignore what's right in front of us because we are frightened of change. Too many times I had told myself that I must work harder at the things I hated, so that I could make the money that came along with it. I had lived someone else's version of life and my soul rejected it, so much so that when it finally got to be too much, my soul screamed for me to WAKE UP. Once you've opened your

---

1   Gabrielle Waxtein, "Famous Women in History: Sarah Bernhardt," Entity Mag (website), posted May 7, 2017, https://www.entitymag.com/famous-women-in-history-sarah-bernhardt/

eyes, heart, mind, and soul to more than you were taught as a child, you can never go back. You can't unknow what you know and nor should you want to. Life has so much more meaning and compassion now.

My journey is still just beginning. The coincidences continue in phenomenal ways everyday. I know each time that I come across a breadcrumb that it is leading to my next destination, where I'm meant to be and I keep moving forward. The proof has been overwhelming. Unknown energy is all around us just waiting to be embraced; it's drawing you closer to your ideal partner; it's creating a path to uncover and transform your pain; and waiting to tell you everything you've ever wanted to know about yourself. Dive deep into the dark corners that you've been hiding from the world. My white flag was a surrender to myself; in the deepest moments of despair I had lived with a husband who nearly took his own life, a seven figure debt that seemed impossible to get out of, and anxiety so debilitating that it clouded my judgement and sabotaged my life. When I let my ego die and proclaimed that I will no longer persecute myself for being different, my entire life shifted. I let go of the resistance to myself and emerged stronger than I ever thought possible. The hopeless situation that suffocated my freedom, all of a sudden became a success story; one that gave me deep compassion for others and a heart to serve. In a few short months everything changed; the debt was gone and we owned two beautiful properties that were beyond our wildest dreams, completely free and clear. I had a husband who was himself again, he was happy, and most of all, my course had been corrected. I was on my true path.

You can't find your way out of the maze by staring at the wall in front of you. That wall will stand still in your path until you move, once you gain a higher perspective, you will see the clear route out. You just have to trust in your ability to pick yourself up and make that first move. If you don't have enough strength, then send out your beacon signal; launch a rock of curiosity and openness to receive, to propel your next move. The right people will show up at exactly the right time if you just have faith that they will. Stay alert to the signs, they are everywhere. Love yourself more than anyone else. Do not compromise your life to ease the pain of someone else's. Speak your truth despite your fear and embrace your hidden gifts because behind that wall you've built to protect your heart is a beautiful infinite source of power that is waiting to be called on. So who is your Sarah? Have you found them yet?

Chapter Fourteen

KARMIC DEBT

"sacred life pattern"

When did I receive the gift of sensing energy? A question pondered years ago. Feeling the physical effects of shadow energy in my recent years, it was present then. As a child, being drawn to the basement to sit with the spirit of a woman, it was present then. Feeling connected to the traditions and ceremonies of other cultures, it was present before my lifetime in this body. There was still much to explore about my ancestral lineage and the gifts passed down upon me. It was becoming clear that these gifts were meant to be uncovered to allow me to communicate with those beyond our physical reality.

A repeating pattern had emerged in my life. During the times when something odd occurred, like an object moving on its own or hearing something strange outside, I was receiving a message. As my claircognizant or *clear knowing* ability improved, I was able to pick up on the energy of someone who had passed on. In most cases I was more like a conduit, where another person received a message they needed, but I hadn't really accepted that maybe some of those messages were meant for me. This became more clear when the messengers didn't leave. It would be like a nagging thought or feeling, like when you know you've forgotten something, but you're not quite sure what.

In Numerology, numbers are used to calculate one's "Life Path Number" and "Destiny Number." The system practiced by ancient Greek philosopher and mathematician, Pythagoras, is commonly used today for the teachings of modern numerology. His beliefs on the interconnectivity of numbers and the energetic vibrations they offer has shaped the practice we use today. Your Life Path Number reveals a hidden purpose to your journey in this lifetime. This number illuminates your strengths, unique talents, and weaknesses that show up

for you as you grow—often exposing why events have occured and what's to come in the future. Your Destiny Number
provides key insight to how your life path will unfold; the
expression of your purpose.[1]

My Life Path Number is eleven. A master number, considered to hold an intense and powerful energy. People who
have a master number in their sign are said to have high intuition and special gifts; an old soul. Representing a connection
to the unconscious and a heightened ability to see the future.
Those who are connected to eleven may experience anxiety
and intense fear if they do not concentrate their efforts.[2] A
shadow side of mine that I had intimately known. A master
number of eleven in a life path reveals a purpose to heal with
heightened psychic abilities. These gifts often appear after difficult life experiences where the development of these extra-
sensory abilities were a necessity.

My Destiny Number is nine, another indicator of an old
soul. The Nines have a mission to reach higher consciousness
and aid others with spiritual enlightenment. We have an ability to connect the dots where a large volume of information
exists.[3] Something I had felt was happening on a grand scale
for some time within my life. In numerology it is believed
that when we enter into this lifetime we choose our birth date
according to the karmic lessons or debts we need to resolve.[4]
So why had I learned this information now, at this point in

1   Aliza Kelly Faragher, "The Basics of Numerology: How to Calculate Your Life
Path and Destiny Numbers,"
allure (website), posted April 10, 2020, https://www.allure.com/story/numerolo-
gy-how-to-calculate-life-path-destiny-number
2   Janey Davies, "What Are Master Numbers and How Do They Affect You?"
Learning Mind, posted June 10, 2017, https://www.learning-mind.com/mas-
ter-numbers/
3   Faragher, "Basics of Numerology," . . .
4   Ann Perry, "Life Path Number," Ann Perry Numerologist (website), posted
July 18, 2018, https://annperrynumerologist.com/resources-1/2018/7/18/life-
path-number

my life, and not before when it may have helped me to decipher what was going on? At this point it was a further assurance of the truth, that the pull I was feeling to spiritual work had a purpose. If I had known this before I may not have had a natural progression to my insights, and instead tried to force something before it's time. My gifts had opened up to me in times of great challenge. The sequence in which I embraced them was in perfect timing.

As I neared closer to the completion of this book, I had an overwhelming feeling of importance to once again examine the history of the property I once owned. This time from a different perspective—with a metaphysical lens. Could a karmic debt attach to a land mass? Would this explain my intuition years earlier to perform the water ceremony on the land? Was there a pull of light and dark happening beneath the surface that was felt in moments of despair through a psychic ability? Karmic debt is like any other debt. It requires a payment and exists to balance out the wrongdoings of a past life. It's a delicate dance of energy that evens out over one's existence.[5] It's a chance to balance the scales and ground the experience within our soul to take forward. What had happened on the land of the lake house to urge this feeling and who was the woman pulling for my attention? The dots were connecting in my mind like sparks over a fire. A grid of information mapped across my higher consciousness and a suggestion emerged.

---

5   Caris Palm Turpen, "The Seven Levels of Karmic Debt," The Michael Teachings, accessed May 27, 2020, https://www.michaelteachings.com/7_levels_karmic_debt.html

"You must find out who experienced a major trauma on this land. Their sorrows are still felt with the Earth. Their cries are heard deep in the night echoing throughout the forest and their body has not been laid to rest."
-A Clairvoyant thought

I had felt that the land was holding onto the energy of a past wrongdoing. This was a secret that had been buried for none to find. But someone didn't realize that cries are not only heard, they are felt and stored within the energetic makeup of our reality. They linger for those who are sensitive to the pulse and wait to be found when the timing is right. An agreement had been made. Long before here and now. Long before the events that lead to this knowing and long before the trauma itself. My higher self had intended on following a path that would lead me down a rabbit hole; one that held the lessons of pain, fear, sorrow, and scarcity; but that would lead me out the other side to the truth of who I was. My heightened intuition and empathic ability was now in tune with a frequency that not only helped those around me, but also connected with those who were left without a voice. I was sensing an energy of those who were cast aside, never to return to this physical life, but who had still left their mark. The mark of their aggressor; karmic debt to be repaid.

The woman in the basement all those years ago, was her soul disturbed when the earth around our home was dug into? Was she just looking for me to help her rest? I was just a child and didn't understand, but it had given me a dot on the map to connect to later on.

I remembered the labyrinth and the strong message I received that day—*red is important.* That red was believed to be the color that spirits could see. A way to draw them home. I recalled my conversation where it was revealed that the donation from the sale of our lake house would be used for the proper care of remains found on private property during new development. Something was intertwined here. A mesh of information. The energy of the land was calling to me, the color red was calling to me, and a faint cry for help from a woman I did not recognize, was calling to me. How could I refuse to listen?

This book is ultimately written for this woman and any other soul who may have left this world in a heightened state of fear or sadness; those who were deemed not important enough to seek justice for, and to honor the families that may still feel the heavy burden of waiting for them to return. My work around my own family trauma led me down a path to connect with the gifts that I had forgotten. Perhaps this woman is still just a reflection of that path, and the healing that happened on every step. A way to honor who I was. I have become more open to learning more about my own ancestry and family lineage. Something that I had previously felt too fearful to do. I feel that we unconsciously carry forth not only the gifts of our loved ones past; our ancestors, but also their hurt, and longing for truth. These pages open up a new trail of breadcrumbs for me. My curiosity in my own family lineage, blood lines and ancestors has sparked a hidden truth in me that is now drawing in answers. My work continues to grow in this field to help others connect the dots, and to advocate for generational healing, not only in our physical reality, but down the lineage of our ancestors that came before. As you read these pages I hope a part of you was drawn here to remember that each and everyone of us are important. You are important and you can make a difference. Fear is felt by all of us and for those who left this world in an elevated state of fear, their energy still lingers in their place for others to feel later. There is hope in the ones that are left and by reading these words you are expanding your thoughts, growing your intuition, and leaning into new possibilities. We are all connected on a much deeper level than we can truly comprehend and I have a feeling that our journey together does not end here. That we will meet again one day. Perhaps aligned on the same cause or maybe again through the words on a page.

This chapter being number fourteen has a significance of its own. It's synchronistic that we would end on this note; fourteen is a karmic debt number. A symbol of "unresolved issues from the past."[6] An intense energy of justice and learning the truth. A blend of determination to share knowledge and examine the deeper meaning beyond the surface. It's a number sending out a beacon seeking help. I don't have all the answers today, but I know that my call will be answered. I will continue to watch for the signs that lead to my next encounter and look for the souls that I'm linked to by destiny, a higher design, and karmic alignment. Perhaps you are one of them, are you curious?

6   "Angel Number 14—Meaning and Symbolism," Angel Number, accessed May 27, 2020, https://angelnumbersmeaning.com/angel-number-14-meaning-and-symbolism/

FULL MOON MEDITATION

The moon is symbolic of natural cycles and a metaphoric renewal of the soul. Representing completion, a full moon holds a heightened state of power, your power. It is a time to reflect on how far you have come. The full moon in its brilliant illumination sheds light on all the shadow aspects of ourselves. This vibrant energy brings the opportunity to clear any heavy emotions of the past and to take another step forward. As you honor where you are in your personal journey, I welcome you to experience a great relaxation, a clearing of stuck and stale energy, and a renewed sense of self.

I encourage you to read this meditation out loud to record on an audio file on your phone or other preferred device. There is hypnotic power in hearing your own voice guide you through this experience. Only listen to your recording when it is safe to relax, and not while operating any heavy machinery or while driving.

Settle in and get comfortable. You may sit or lie down, whichever is most comfortable for you. The goal is to keep your spine straight and your legs and arms uncrossed to allow for your energy to flow freely.

Shall we begin?

Soften your gaze and gently close your eyes.

With a deep breath in through the nose, fill your body with relaxation and comfort. As you breathe out through the mouth, release all stuck and uncomfortable energy. Again, breathe in the nose and out through the mouth. One more time, breathe deep into the belly and release out through the mouth.

Good.

Allow your body to sink into its surroundings and let go of any tension. Continue your breathing, slow and steady. Scan your body now for anywhere you might be holding tension. Focus your attention briefly on each spot and release each muscle.

You are being called to remember that this journey is not meant to cause you struggle or pain. You are open to change and change is good. The steps you take today allow for you to build on new loving energy and to align more and more with the best version of yourself.

Soften the tiny muscles around your eyes, release your jaw, and let your shoulders fall.

As I count down from three, all tension is released and you are ready to clear all that is not serving you.

3 – You are going deeper.
2 – You are more relaxed.
1 – You are safe and well.

You are standing outside amongst the stars—the night is clear, the air is warm; the moon is full and supercharged. In the distance, you notice a flicker of light dancing across the surface of a body of water. The moon light has created a clear direct path to the water's edge. As you walk towards it, you notice a low hum radiating out towards you from the water. Drawing you closer and comforting each step. Mother earth is calling you to reflect in her waters. Each step closer you draw deeper and deeper into the night's calming energy.

You reach the water's edge and as you stand basking in the light of the full moon, you look across the surface to see nothing but wide-open calm waters. Standing here, you look down to see a clear reflection of yourself in the glass-like surface. The image is bright and surrounded by a beautiful glow of white light. Like a halo around your body.

As your eyes gaze deep into the eyes of the image looking back at you, you are one in the same. Connected on a deep cellular level. Focus now softly into the left eye of your self-image. As you gaze deeper and deeper into the image staring back at you, you hear:

You are safe.
You are stronger than you know.
Let go of all that needs to leave. You are loved in this moment, and you are enough.

Look now across the water's surface and allow yourself to walk into the shallow shoreline if it feels right for you to do so. Allow the gentle waters to move fluently across your body. If you prefer to just dip your toes in or sit on the shore that is okay, too. Take in these next few moments with a breath, as the fresh water clears and renews your soul. Allow what needs to shift to flow out and away in the gentle current. You may feel lighter or as if a toxin has been released and washed away.

Now emerge out of the water and stand back up on the shoreline.

Before you turn to head back home, take a moment to recall a feeling of a time that you were thankful for and embrace that feeling again now.

Good.

With a clear head and grateful heart, turn back to head home. On sturdy ground you move forward, taking the short walk back to where you started. Along the path, lit by the moon. In a moment I will guide you back to here and now where you will feel at ease and balanced in the days ahead. Tonight's sleep is deep and restful.

1 – You are ready to return.
2 – You feel the ground beneath you.
3 – You are here, safe, and well.

Take a few moments to wiggle your toes, feel the weight of your body grounded where you sit or lie. When you are ready, slowly open your eyes and allow yourself to adjust back into your space. If you received any thoughts or insights that you want to make note of, take a moment to write them down now.

REVIEWS FOR QUANTUM CHANGE PROCESS SESSIONS:

"I cannot fully explain the transformational shift I experienced during my Quantum Change Process™ session, or the gratitude I feel for Kady for helping me with this. Kady walked me through each step with kindness and reassurance. She listened intently and helped me piece together a story that has been playing unconsciously through my entire life – creating tension, anger and impatience when triggered. While I still have work to do, Kady has set me on a new path in life. One full of hope, control, and joy. I am blessed to have met her. Thank you Kady for your patience, guidance and this positively transformational gift you have given me."

-Becky Moore

"I had suffered with severe anxiety and depression for a large portion of my life and had tried several ways of healing over the years. I had still felt like there was something missing. The effects of my session with Kady were very powerful, and a huge eye opener. Kady was able to narrow in on a specific area of concern for me to shed light on a pattern that had been running and now my entire life makes sense. This has been life changing to find one of the major keys that has been holding me back my entire life. I highly recommend the Quantum Change Process™ to bring to light something that is buried deep inside."

-Jeffrey Saunders

ig: @kady.romagnuolo
fb: @kadymindsetcoach
li: kady-romagnuolo
goodreads: kady-romagnuolo
www.kadymindsetcoach.com

Kady Romagnuolo is a mindset and performance coach who specializes in helping clients work through fear and low self-confidence. As a board certified NLP Master Practitioner and Quantum Change Process™ Practitioner her techniques involve accessing the root cause behind limiting beliefs and negative emotions. Her passion as a coach comes from a place of experience. Kady grew up in a low income suburb of Calgary that was quite rough. Her childhood experiences left her living a life hiding behind a mask. Portraying to the world as a successful Realtor® while hiding her extreme low self-confidence and constant fear that she wasn't good enough.

Today Kady is a recognized professional in her industry. Her workshops and breakthrough programs help individuals conquer self-doubt and to reach their highest potential. As a motivational speaker she helps others to engage their core story and embrace change from within. She lives waterfront on a country estate on the outskirts of Kingston, ON with her husband and two dogs.

GOLDEN BRICK ROAD
PUBLISHING HOUSE

Link arms with us as we pave new paths to a better and more expansive world.

Golden Brick Road Publishing House (GBRPH) is a small, independently initiated boutique press created to provide social-innovation entrepreneurs, experts, and leaders a space in which they can develop their writing skills and content to reach existing audiences as well as new readers.

Serving an ambitious catalogue of books by individual authors, GBRPH also boasts a unique co-author program that capitalizes on the concept of "many hands make light work." GBRPH works with our authors as partners. Thanks to the value, originality, and fresh ideas we provide our readers, GBRPH books are now available in bookstores across North America.

We aim to develop content that effects positive social change while empowering and educating our members to help them strengthen themselves and the services they provide to their clients.

Iconoclastic, ambitious, and set to enable social innovation, GBRPH is helping our writers/partners make cultural change one book at a time.

Inquire today at www.goldenbrickroad.pub